Prestel Museum Guide

Schloss Wilhelmshöhe
Kassel

The Collection of Antiquities
The Old Masters Art Gallery
The Collection of Prints
and Drawings

D1614379

Prestel

Munich · London · New York

© Prestel Verlag
Munich · London · New York, 2000

© for works illustrated: by the Staatliche Museen
Kassel; Verwaltung der Staatlichen Schlösser and
Gärten, Bad Homburg v.d.H. (pp. 182–188); by
the artists, their heirs or assigns, with the excep-
tion of Jean Dubuffet and Wols, by VG Bild-Kunst,
Bonn, 2000; Georg Baselitz by Georg Baselitz;
Erich Heckel by the Estate of Erich Heckel,
Hemmenhofen; Ernst Ludwig Kirchner by Inge-
borg and Dr. Wolfgang Henze, Wichtrach/Bern;
and Ernst Wilhelm Nay with E. Nay-Scheibler

© the plans on the front and back flaps:
Staatliche Museen Kassel, using plans
by the Atelier 44 für Visuelle Kommunikation
Homann-Güner-Blum, Hanover
Photographs: Staatliche Museen Kassel (G. Bößert,
U. Brunzel, M. Büsing, A. Hensmanns, E. Müller,
U. Reuschling)
Front flap: Rembrandt, *Saskia van Uylenburgh in
Profile*, c. 1634–42, cf. p. 148
Back flap: Schloss Wilhelmshöhe, Kassel:
view from the west
p. 12: *Victoria*, c. 150 AD, detail of illus. p. 51
p. 60: Hans Baldung, *Hercules and Antaeus*, 1531,
detail from illus. on p. 73
p. 160: Johann Liss, *Morra Players in an Osteria
Garden*, c. 1620, detail from illus. p. 171
p. 181: Ballhaus, interior view
p. 182: Weissenstein Wing: View from the west

Staatliche Museen Kassel
Management, Administration, PR
Schloss Wilhelmshöhe
34131 Kassel
Tel.: (561) 9377-7
Fax: (561) 9377-666
www.uni-kassel.de/museum/
and www.museum-kassel.hessen.de

Schloss Wilhelmshöhe
Opening Hours

Collection of Antiquities:
Tuesday–Sunday: 10am–5pm
Closed Mondays

The Old Masters Art Gallery:
Tuesday–Friday: 10am–5pm
Closed Mondays

The Collection of Prints and Drawings
Mondays–Fridays: 9am–12pm

Ballhaus: April–October
Tuesday–Sunday: 10am–5pm
Closed Mondays

Weissenstein Wing, Herkules-Oktogon
Grosses Gewächshaus, Löwenburg:
See pp. 182–187

Translated from the German by
Almuth Seebohm, Munich

Prestel Verlag
Mandlstrasse 26, 80802 Munich,
Tel.: +49 (89) 38 17 09-0
Fax: +49 (89) 38 17 09-35;
4 Bloomsbury Place, London WC1A 2QA
Tel.: +44 (020) 7323-5004
Fax: +44 (020) 7636-8004;
175 Fifth Avenue, Suite 402,
New York, NY 10010
Tel.: +1 (212) 995-2720
Fax: +1 (212) 995-2733
www.prestel.com

*Die Deutsche Bibliothek CIP-Einheits-
Aufnahme* data is available
ISBN 3-7913-2374-1

Design and Layout: G.Pfeifer, Germering
Typesetting: EDV-Fotsatz Huber, Germering
Printing and binding: Passavia Druck-
service GmbH, Passau
Lithography: ReproLine, Munich

Printed in Germany on acid-free paper
ISBN 3-7913-2374-1

Texts by:
Peter Gercke (PG), Margot Klee (MK),
Hans-Jörg Czech (HJC), Jürgen M. Lehmann
(JML), Bernhard Schnackenburg (BS),
Christiane Lukatis (CL), Stefanie Heckmann
(SH), Ursula Brossette (UB)

Contents

A New Museum for Old Collections

On the slope of Habichtswald above the city of Kassel in the north of the State of Hesse lies an historically grown ensemble that is one of the most important cultural sites in Germany. Almost like the Acropolis, it is crowned by a gigantic monumental statue of Hercules towering above the rocky cliff. Before him spreads the tripartite palace like a temple, sheltering the marble figures of gods and many paintings. It was a felicitous and right decision when the provincial government of Hesse voted in 1960 to house both the collection of antiquities and the collection of old master paintings in Schloss Wilhelmshöhe. The antiquities had been removed from their 'ancestral home' in the Museum Fridericianum, where they had been exhibited up until 1913. The paintings, formerly in the gallery building that was destroyed by bombs in 1943, were also 'homeless.' The central tract of the palace, which had been gutted by fire in 1945, became the new home for the two collections. Thus the Neo-Classical palace dating from 1800 acquired new content. Blending in with the naturally designed landscape park on the hill, it has proven to be a success ever since it was opened in 1974.

From 1994 on, however, one section of the museum in the palace after another had to be closed because of serious structural defects endangering the works of art on display in the central tract. The poorly insulated lean-to roof and the unheated window niches caused so much condensation to collect from the humid air in the galleries that the frames of the paintings were fitted with projecting metal sheets to protect them from dripping water.

The planning for a complete renovation was launched in 1994 with a limited architectural competition for a new roof for the main building. Right from the start, the vote favoured the design by the Munich architect Stephan Braunfels. He proposed a lantern storey, vertically glazed on all sides and topped with a gable roof, in order to direct daylight into the high third storey.

The proposal fell victim to the Kasselers' disapproval of this 'greenhouse' solution and, finally, to a political veto in 1995. Planning came to a standstill while attempts were made to lower the height of the lantern storey. The ceiling height of over 4.5 metres required for major works and large-scale formats was to be attained by creating an inner central gallery two storeys high, lit by natural daylight from above.

By December 1995 a consensus, if not full, could be reached on the outer form and the interior design between the architect, building authorities, the ministries of finance and of science and art, the city of Kassel and, last but not least, the demands of the museum curators. We proceeded from the historically based concept of a gable roof. Under it, taking full advantage of the height prescribed by the apexes of the gables of the two historic porticoes, there was room to insert an attic storey. With central galleries lit from the tops of the outer walls, flanked on either side by lower cabinets lit from above, the new storey is like a basilica in cross section.

Other objectives of the renovation included converting the lower storey on the well-lit valley side of the palace into a service area for visitors. It now houses hitherto non-existent information and service facilities such as a foyer, cloakrooms, the museum shop and a bistro. The storage areas were thus reduced to a minimum. A seldom-used lecture hall was replaced by an auditorium with 40 seats in the north exedra of the third storey. Furthermore, the three central and peripheral staircases and lift shafts were removed. Instead, two new access routes run vertically through and facing the exedras at the far ends of the central tract. Thus a straightforward itinerary through the museum now begins at the south exedra with its semicircular staircase. Four different floor plans for the four storeys of galleries were custom-made depending on the exhibits in order to show the works of art to their best advantage. Ancient art is presented in a large open hall lined with pillars, interrupted by two staircases in the centre, and in the adjacent wing. With an area of 17 x 61 metres, the hall fills the ground floor of the entire central tract, making its vast dimensions perceptible.

The art gallery begins upstairs on the first floor with rooms aligned on two axes forming one itinerary. The rooms on the well-lit side facing the valley are deeper than those on the darker side facing the high horizon of the hill. Thus the same amount of light falls on all the inner walls. The centre of this storey features the Flora Room, occupying the full depth of the building, its dimensions allowing van der Werff's ceiling paintings of the "Apotheosis of Flora" to be hung on the ceiling. It also serves as a small concert and lecture hall. The plan of the second floor, which has a lower ceiling, is determined by a series of small cabinets all around the outside. Their slightly angled side walls trap the daylight and direct it towards the paintings. The shallow depth of the cabinets corresponds to the small size of the windows so as to maximise the intensity of the light falling on the walls opposite. This leaves room for a large gallery down the full length of the middle of the building. It has artificial light and can be subdivided by means of sliding doors concealed in the walls. This makes it a suitable exhibition space for the State Museums' Collection of Prints and Drawings, where drawings and graphic art that would be damaged by daylight can be displayed. Here, as on all other floors of the gallery, the buttress system of Posenenske's earlier restoration is now within the walls. The pillars have thus become invisible.

Finally, the third floor is distinguished by the completely new rooftop structure covering the entire central tract. Further development by Stephan Braunfels transformed the basic idea of the gable roof into a mansard roof, allowing the original balustrade crowning the attic to remain silhouetted against the sky. Inside, a concealed loft made of upright panels of opaque glass runs all around the top of each of the five central rooms. Daylight filters into the lofts from the sloped glazing of the mansard roof. The top of the roof and the ceilings of the rooms are self-contained units to keep out the heat and extreme brightness of the noonday sun. The place for the air conditioning system could therefore continue to be used economically and power costs kept low. Thanks to the architect's newly developed structure, the central rooms and the eight adjacent low cabinets with their translucent ceilings are lit by natural and evenly distributed daylight. The quality of daylight thus obtained does justice to the major works of 17th-century painting on exhibit, to which a continuous central axis, in the manner of a triumphal way, provides visual and physical access. Visitors can reach all storeys via the semi-circular stairway in the south exedra and passenger lifts facing it. When attendance is high, the large goods lift at the other end of the building can also be used to relieve crowding. For the first time since 1944 there is once again a passageway on the ground-floor level to the Weissenstein wing, where the late 18th-century rooms of the palace with their impressive Empire and Restoration interiors have been preserved.

The interior decoration of the newly developed galleries aimed for calm clear walls to match the orderly symmetrical subdivisions of the floor plan. It was to provide a quiet backdrop for the sculptural and tonal values of the works of art, which can thus create their own effects. Bright and restless decorative features were therefore out of the question. Grey lava tiles and low-key oak parquet laid with plain boards create an homogeneous flooring harmonising with the walls painted a light slate-grey. For the first-floor rooms and the third-floor cabinets of the art gallery a lightly glazed coat of paint in earthen hues of Venetian red or sienna green was chosen. It is to counteract excessive luminance on the walls lest they overpower the relatively dark oil paintings.

The artificial lighting was planned by the Kunst-Licht-Kunst firm of Berlin, who succeeded in implementing an unprecedented solution with recessed fittings along narrow channels in the ceiling panels. Despite occupying only a minimum amount of space, the opaque energy-efficient tubes shine by means of reflectors on most of the wall spaces with an even incidence of light. The quality of the light shows both the yellow-red and the blue-green spectrum in the pictures to full advantage. Selected artificial lighting is installed throughout to brighten and supplement the incidence and colour of the daylight. With its regular opening hours from 10 a.m. to 5 p.m., Schloss Wilhelmshöhe is considered to be mainly a daylight museum. The artificial lighting is understood as a necessary supplement on dark days.

The museum architecture's aim was to serve the works of art and to display them in the given framework under the best conditions for viewing and to their best advantage. Additional features were included in the belief that positive and well-designed rooms provide a better setting for works of art than a neutralised series of spaces. They affirm the beauty of the simplest materials. The 'dome dispute,' initiated by a group of Kassel citizens and monuments preservationists committed to cultural history who advocated the reconstruction of lost parts of the building, had little effect on the planning. The reconstruction of the half-timbered dome, completely destroyed in 1945, and a drum to support it would have entailed many disadvantages for the museum. Funding had never been available. Moreover, the tried and true principle of monuments conservationists and of all restorations is "to preserve and not to reconstruct." A solution that would reduce the ceiling light illuminating the precious paintings would have been seriously detrimental. A time lag of many years would have come about through renewed fund-raising and complicated new planning. As it is, the Art Gallery had already been closed for six years and the Collection of Antiquities for three.

Schloss Wilhelmshöhe, built 1791–1801 by the Kassel court architects Du Ry and Jussow, has proven a superb museum site. The renovation will help the museum to serve its purpose better than ever.

The present brief guide in the Prestel series of museum guides presents a selection of major works from the collections of antiquities, old master paintings, and prints and drawings. The short descriptions sum up research and interpretations concerning the most important pieces in the state museums. What the architecture, an architecture of light throughout, tries to do for viewing the works of art, the guide tries to do for understanding them by providing basic orientation and art historical concepts. As testimonies of long-lost and forgotten civilisations, the works of art reach over into to our times. In their non-verbal, commonly understandable language, they can evoke with their figures and perceptions something that is

threatening to turn into a shadow kingdom due to the prevailing lack of education in European cultural traditions. The museum can try to bring some of this to light as far as form and content are concerned. "Myth and cosmology teach us: when developments have reached their lowest point, it is time to turn around." (Schwanitz 1999)

Finally, we would like to thank everyone who made a fresh start for Schloss Wilhelmshöhe possible, for their commitment beyond the call of duty to this great project. The Museum Association did everything to get the restoration of the three van der Werff ceiling paintings underway. They were actively supported by the Patrons' Circle. We also succeeded in having the monumental painting by Roos of "The Menagerie of Landgrave Carl" restored.

Patrons' support also made the purchase of display cabinets and seating possible. Where everything had always been expected to come from the state, the awakening of patronage for public art property was an unusual and decisive step.

Dr. Hans Ottomeyer
Director of the State Museums Kassel
(1995–2000)

A Brief History of Schloss Wilhelmshöhe and Park

Gerd Fenner

The palace and the landscape park of Wilhelmshöhe were developed during the first years of the reign of the Hessian Landgrave Wilhelm IX (1785–1821), later to become the Prince Elector Wilhelm I.

As early as 1606 to 1610, Landgrave Moritz (1596–1627) had had a palatial hunting lodge erected on this site of the Augustinian nunnery of Weissenstein, secularised in 1526. Small landscaped gardens and a grotto had completed the architecture.

It was only after a lengthy pause that new measures were undertaken at the end of the 17th century. They resulted in one of the great highlights of garden art in Europe: "the grandest design combining architecture and landscape ever dared anywhere in the Baroque era" (Georg Dehio). Inspired by Italian gardens dating from the period around 1600, Landgrave Karl (1677–1730) had the Roman artist Giovanni Francesco Guerniero (*c.* 1665–1745) create a concept for a water axis that was, compared to the Italian prototypes, expanded to gigantic proportions. Descending from an octagon crowning a slope of the Habichtswald, a monumental cascade subdivided by numerous grottoes, terraces, pools and squares was to lead down to the new palace planned at the base of 'Karl's Mountain.' However, only the upper third, with the octagon, was realised. Once the monumental statue of the Farnese Hercules was set up to top it in 1717, construction was discontinued. The designs for the palace, which the ambitious princely client had had designed by Guerniero, Louis Remy de la Fosse, Johann Friedrich Karcher and Alessandro Rossini, also remained unrealised. With the characteristic self-assurance of a Baroque ruler, the landgrave had Guerniero's general plan published in an album of engravings, "Delineatio montis," by well known Roman printmakers to propagate his own fame.

The influence of the English garden style was incorporated under the auspices of Landgrave Friedrich II (1760–1785), who devoted his attention to the grounds of Weissenstein after the Seven Years' War. A number of traditional elements were set up along the main axis in front of the palace, including a bowling green and a fountain in a large, symmetrically shaped pool surrounded by a wooden triumphal arch and a pergola. The areas on either side of the Baroque axis, on the other hand, acquired a series of small garden spaces with sham buildings, some with wooden sculptures of ancient poets and philosophers to evoke certain moods and atmospheres. In the 'Chinese' village of Mulang, of which several buildings are still preserved, there was also a 'Turkish mosque.' This was clearly a reference to Kew Gardens in London by William Chambers.

The picturesque Anglo-Chinese garden was enhanced in horticultural terms by the planting of over 400 species of trees and shrubs collected in Europe, Asia and America. The hunting lodge-palace built by Landgrave Moritz was rebuilt and enlarged by Landgrave

Friedrich in the 60s. Two decades later he commissioned the French architect Charles De Wailly (1730–1798), widely known in his day, to design a representative country palace. The death of the landgrave in 1785, however, put an end to the planning. His son and heir, Wilhelm IX (1785–1821) began immediately upon his accession with redesigning the gardens into a landscape garden in the latest English fashion. This talented princely amateur architect collaborated with the architects Simon Louis Du Ry (1726–1799) and Heinrich Chistoph Jussow (1754–1825) as well as the court gardener Daniel August Schwarzkopf. The famous garden theorist Christian Cay Lorenz Hirschfeld (1742–1792), who had been offered the post of chief gardener in Kassel, followed the developments in the new park and probably contributed many an idea.

The grounds were to be given a magnificent, stately and heroic character. As the court gardener Daniel August Schwarzkopf put it in 1793 after completion of the major part of the project: "Everything that was built harmonises with the landscape and is realised in a heroic and grand style." As the Baroque buildings in the upper part of the park were granted to possess this effect, they could be integrated into the new general concept. However, the symmetrically shaped parts and Landgrave Friedrich's various small structures were largely removed: "The entire crew of wooden gods was retired in one day and stored in the staghounds' stable" (Schwarzkopf 1791). Natural-looking landscape views and plantings appeared in their stead. A complex network of winding pathways provided access to changing views and perspectives. To augment the effect, the small brooks were turned into a large one with a lot of variations, running from the cascade to the lake. Especially effective was the staging of the aqueduct Jussow built in 1788–1792, from which masses of water plunged into a deep ravine. The counterpart to this 'Roman' ruin was the Löwenburg (Lion's

Johann Heinrich Bleuler, View of Schloss Wilhelmshöhe across the lake, 1825

Heinrich Chistoph Jussow, Design for the central tract of Schloss Wilhelmshöhe, 1791

Castle, 1793–1800). Planned simply as a picturesque ruin of a tower with an adjacent building, it soon developed into a complex compound in the shape of a ruin around an inner court. The meaning of the structure, which is one of the earliest Neo-Gothic works in Germany, extended far beyond that of a piece of sham architecture. Wilhelm IX chose it for his tomb; in 1821 he was buried in the crypt under the chapel.

At the same time as the changes in the gardens, the planning for a new palace had got underway. At first only a small building was projected overlooking the lake to one side of the park's central axis. After the demolition of various wings of the old hunting lodge-palace, the construction of a solitary building began in June 1786 under Simon Louis Du Ry. It has survived as today's Weissenstein Wing. Combining a base course storey with a colossal order of three-dimensional columns, it was oriented on English Palladian country houses. Du Ry was able to prevail over Wilhelm IX's wish for a ruin-like exterior by giving it an intact Neo-Classical facade. As early as 1787, the project in progress seemed too small to the landgrave and he felt that it required an identical building opposite and, finally, a central tract between the two. Joining them in the planning and construction of these sections was Heinrich Chistoph Jussow, whom the landgrave had hired as a building inspector in 1788 specifically for this purpose. Jussow was in charge of the construction of the two wings, where his designs for the rooms in the Weissenstein wing and the chapel in the church wing have been preserved to this day. In developing the numerous versions of the *corps de logis* (central tract) requested by Wilhelm IX, Jussow eventually became the competitor of his superior and former teacher Du Ry. Wilhelm IX vacillated for a long time between different solutions, which included a ruin and a triumphal arch. Finally in 1791, he decided in favour of Jussow's design, which best corresponded to his ideas of monumental and sublime architecture. A massive portico with Ionic columns three storeys high and a pediment, as well as a dome on a drum based on the Pantheon in Rome, picked up elements of revolutionary architecture and enhanced the impact of the central tract with respect to the wings as well as the landscape.

The construction and interior decoration were completed in 1802. The landgrave took the completion of the facade in 1798 as an opportunity to rename the palace Wilhelmshöhe. The *corps de logis* housed the prince's apartment on the ground floor and two others on the *bel-étage* (first floor) for high-ranking visitors. The two-storey banqueting hall was also located here.

As early as the period of the kingdom of Westphalia (1807–1813) of which Kassel was the seat of the court, King Jérôme Bonaparte had some of the rooms redecorated in the Empire style. North of the palace, Leo von Klenze built the theatre in 1810, converted into a ballroom by Johann Conrad Bromeis in 1828–1830.

A major alteration to the palace was made under Prince Elector Wilhelm II, who had the three separate wings linked by means of connecting structures, giving the palace today's massive appearance. Interventions in the park initiated by Wilhelm II included the final major expansion of the fountains by means of a new waterfall set up by the inspector of the fountains, Karl Steinhofer. A huge greenhouse erected in 1822 by Bromeis was one of the earliest glass-and-iron structures in Germany.

After the Electorate of Hesse was annexed by Prussia in 1866, Wilhelmshöhe became a centre of attention during the residence of two emperors. From September 1870 to March 1871 the French Emperor Napoleon III, captured after the battle of Sedan, was put up here. From 1889 to 1918 the German Emperor Wilhelm II's family came every year to spend the summer in Wilhelmshöhe. The palace, which had come under the authority of the Prussian palace administration in 1918, was severely damaged when bombed on 19 January 1945. While the scarcely affected wings could soon be restored, the gutted central tract long remained a ruin.

It was finally reconstructed along with the chapel wing and the connecting tract from 1968 to 1974. Having been found suitable for a museum, the building was emptied of its core and rebuilt according to plans by Paul Posenenske. The reconstruction of the dome was decided against because of the palace's new use.

Serious structural defects required that the art gallery be closed in 1994. The partial restoration originally contemplated was to be replaced by comprehensive measures for new rooms in the entire central tract. The architect Stephan Braunfels was commissioned to realise the project. In June 2000 the Old Masters Art Gallery and the Collection of Antiquities could be reopened.

The History of the Collection

Peter Gercke

The Collection of Antiquities of the Landgraves of Hesse-Kassel from 1603 to 1866

The earliest documentary evidence for the collecting of antiquities by the landgraves of Hesse-Kassel records the purchase of antiquities from France, including seven Roman lamps, by Landgrave Moritz ('The Learned,' who reigned 1592–1627) for his 'cabinet of antiquities' in 1603. Moritz had first been introduced to ancient sites and collections of antiquities in 1602 during a trip to Paris to visit King Henri IV. Ever since the Renaissance, European rulers and scholars had been amassing ancient artefacts, objects relating to natural science, scientific instruments, tools, models and libraries in their cabinets of art and curiosities (known as Kunstkammer and Wunderkammer). Laboratories and workshops often completed such collections. This microcosm, individual, personal and capable of being handled by one person alone, served as an illustration of the world in theory and practice.

At the height of Absolutism in the Baroque era, Landgrave Karl (reign 1670–1730) steadily expanded the collection and had it looked after by an 'antiquarius.' It was moved into separate buildings: one house for the sculptures, minor arts, coins, and jewellery, housing a 'sculptura' cabinet and a cabinet of antiquities, and another for the models. There was a growing interest in seeing archaeological finds from Italy and Greece in person as

well as in acquiring finds through archaeological digs at home. Hessian troops brought ancient statuettes, coins and marble reliefs to their sovereign in 1687–88 upon their return from Greece. On an educational journey in 1699–1700, Karl personally bought coins, gems, cameos, casts, etc. in Italy, where he hit upon the inspiration for his Baroque architectural projects and for the interior decoration of his residence.

Partial to the art and civilisation of Classical antiquity, Landgrave Friedrich II (reign 1760–1785), in the spirit of the Age of Enlightenment and Neo-Classicism, collected mainly Roman, Etruscan, Egyptian and Greek antiquities, copies, models and casts. He founded academies and in 1779 set up the Museum Fridericianum (its motto: "docent et oblectant" means "they teach and delight"), a temple of the muses complete with library for scholarly research and education that was European in rank and encyclopaedic in scope. The landgrave owed his views on ancient art – particularly sculpture – as being exemplary and worthy of imitation to Johann Joachim Winckelmann (1717–1768). Winckelmann's art historical doctrine attributed the highest rank to ancient Athens. According to him, the Greeks had attained to "noble simplicity and quiet grandeur" because "liberty alone was the reason for the power and majesty that Athens achieved."

Kassel took almost no part in the developments in scholarship and archaeological museums from the end of the 18th century through most of the 19th. The landgraves, who numbered among the prosperous German princes, no longer contributed to the advancement of their ancestral collection and related scholarly research from 1785 to 1866. A self-sufficient middle class, which could have made up for the aristocratic owners' lack of interest with cultural and financial commitment of their own, was not yet in existence.

The State Collection of the Prussian Province of Hesse-Nassau up to 1945

With the contractual annexation of the landgraviate by the Prussian government in 1866, the collection became yet another part of a royal provincial museum. Its contents were regarded as complete and to serve educational purposes alone. Only plaster casts of sculptures in other collections of originals could be added to the casts acquired in the 18th century. Not until 1887 did a modest expansion begin, with occasional purchases but mainly gifts and loans. As the Berlin government did not grant any funding to develop the 18th-century core collection of large and small-sized marble and bronze sculptures, the museum administration tried at least sporadically to expand the collection of vases and terracottas. This art form, central to research, discoveries and collecting trends in the 19th century, had been entirely lacking in the early Neo-Classical core collection.

In order to rouse the royal provincial museum from its partly culpable, partly decreed dormancy, and to bring it

up to date with general developments in museums in the 19th century, the Hessisches Landesmuseum was founded and opened in 1913. It embraced the collections of archaeology, minor arts, crafts, and history of technology. Its educational objectives referred expressly to the grand concept of the Museum Fridericianum of 1799. However, in matters of furnishings, collection expansion and effectiveness, it was not able to emulate the example of its prototype. For the collection of antiquities the major accomplishment to result from this step was the housing in the central hall (Antikensaal) and the publication of the exemplary catalogue of ancient sculptures and bronzes in 1915.

In order to obtain more of a profile as well as a more decorative and less soberly educational presentation compared to other German museums, the state cultural and historical collections were merged with others (some that had remained in the possession of the Hessian landgraves in 1866 and some acquired by the Landgrave Philipp of Hesse since the 20s) to form the Landgraves' Museum (1935–1939). After their installation in the renovated historic building was completed in 1939, the museum's contents were hurriedly packed up by command and evacuated just before World War II began.

The State Collection of the Land of Hesse since 1945

After the war, the ancient minor arts were recovered from storage in the cellars of the ruined 'Galerie an der Schönen Aussicht' building of 1875 and the ancient sculptures from the cellars of Schloss Wilhelmshöhe, which had likewise been destroyed. The collection, now having passed into the possession of the Land of Hesse, was accessible from 1948 on and some of it was provisionally exhibited in the Museum of the Land of Hesse (Hessisches Landesmuseum). A conservation division of the museum's own, however, is lacking to this day. Nevertheless, ever since 1961 the collection has been growing modestly every year.

After the collection of antiquities was set up in Schloss Wilhelmshöhe in 1974, the most important accessions up to 1980 were in the form of magnificent loans from the Peter and Irene Ludwig Collection (Aachen) since 1965 and the Paul Dierichs Collection (Kassel) since 1974. Integrated into the context of the state collection and recent donations since 1975, they have been on view to the public. Thanks to the generous kindness of the collectors, the museum was able to obtain these works on loan and fit them in purposefully with regard to the historic structure of the collection.

Kassel's collection policy is oriented on the historic core collection, on contemporary socio-political objectives, and on the research and methods of the science of archaeology. This encyclopaedic and educational task calls for making the encounter with ancient art and civilisation understandable to the general public by illustrating it with archaeological monuments and documents, to which originals, copies, replicas, models, re-constructions and information all contribute.

Egypt

0–31st dynasty,
about 3100–332 BC

Pantheon

22nd–26th dynasty, 945–525 BC
bronze, cast, incised decoration
L 21.5, H 22 cm – Inv. no. Br 6
found in a tomb near Memphis (?)
purchased 1780

Thoth, the god of the moon and of
wisdom, sits on a throne with a row of
lower Egyptian gods in front of him
on the left, and upper Egyptian ones
on the right. The ibis-headed god in
a wig wears the Atef crown (ram's
horns, bulrush crown with a disk of
the sun or moon, flanked by ostrich
feathers and uraeus snakes with a disk
of the sun on either side) and originally held the sceptre of Was in his
left fist. Baboons and falcons sit on the
armrests. An ibis is perched on a pedestal in the centre. In front of it there
was originally a small standing figure
of the donor. Many other gods, a pharaoh and inscriptions are engraved on
almost all sides of this group of Egyp-

tian gods (pantheon) with the largest
number of figures. Dating it to the
22nd to 26th dynasty is further suggested by the patronymic Osorkon in
the donor's inscription. Thoth was
worshipped in the late period as an
all-Egyptian king and creator god.   PG

Isis and Horus

25th dynasty – Ptolemaic period,
775–30 BC
bronze, cast, H 20.7 cm – Inv. no. Br 1
purchased 1750

Enthroned Isis is nursing her son
Horus-Harpocrates, who is sitting on
her lap. The divine mother is dressed
in a close-fitting gown that emphasises
the curving shapes of her elongated
body. She wears a wig with a vulture's
hood and the distinctive crown, consisting of a wreath of snakes, cow's
horns and the disk of the sun. Her
nude son is characterised by his braid-
like Horus curl as the heir of his

father Osiris, the mythical ruler of Egypt. Preserved on the base are the remains of the donor's hieroglyphic inscription. This high-quality group shows a motif that was a particular favourite in the late Egyptian period. The cult of Isis, documented as early as in the Old Kingdom, was a widespread mystery cult during the Greek and Roman period throughout the entire Mediterranean region. Whether the Egyptian image of the mother of god influenced the Christian one of the Madonna and Child is the subject of controversy.   *PG*

Ushabti of Wah-ib-Re-em-achtet

26th–30th dynasty, 664–343 BC
silica ceramic, H 14.9cm – Inv. no.V 3
purchased before 1785

This ushabti with a wig and ceremonial beard of the late period is carrying a hoe, hand plough, and bag of seeds ready for work in the fields. His name testifies to the posthumous cult of the pharaohs Psammetich I and Apries of the 26th dynasty (664–525 BC).

Small mummy-shaped ushabtis were grave-goods. They were to preserve the image of the dead. As they adapt the image of Osiris they also embody hope for immortality. Later re-interpretations assigned them the function of surrogates, servants or slaves to perform tasks for the deceased in the kingdom of the dead. Ideally, the deceased had 365 ushabtis – one for each day of the year – complete with the necessary overseers.

Siliceous figurines of this kind were produced serially with moulds. The ancient Egyptians called the shiny glazed ceramic (so-called 'Egyptian faience') "the luminous, radiant material." In it they saw both the azure of the sky and the green of the vegetation as well as the bluish green of the water, colour and luminosity standing for life-giving forces and the eternal cycle of divinely inspired nature.   *PG*

Asia Minor, Troy

Bronze Age, 2500–1100 BC

Cup

2600–2400 BC; Early Bronze Age
early Trojan I
clay, H 7.4 cm – Inv. no.T 807
purchased in Turkey around 1960
gift of Oskar Liebeck 1984

The globular cup without a base has a short constricted neck and a flared rim. The ribbon handle is attached at the widest part of the body and joins

This slender funnel-shaped beaker has two projecting, bow-shaped, loop handles. Their lower ends are attached above the flat base, the upper ends just below the rim. The surface of this hand-made and formerly colour-coated vessel is smoothed out in long vertical strips resembling those on metal vessels.

This early Bronze Age form common in Anatolia and Greek regions has been identified with the "depas amphikypellon" (two-handled beaker) mentioned by Homer. *PG*

the upper rim of the lip. The body is ribbed with vertical grooves. This hand-made, handy little drinking vessel was coated with a paint slip before firing, and the surface was burnished before firing. In the Early Bronze Age monochrome terracotta with a metallic lustre predominated in the eastern Mediterranean and Anatolia over vessels with painted ornament. The red colour and burnished surface are thought to be in imitation of new metal prototypes, mainly of copper and bronze. *PG*

Cyprus

Bronze Age, 2500–1150 BC
Early Iron Age, 1100–600 BC

Beaker

2500–2000 BC; Early Bronze Age
from Troy II-V
clay, H 15 cm – Inv. no. ALg 107
on loan from the Schliemann collection
since 1914

Jug

1750–1600 BC;
Middle Bronze Age
clay, burnished, relief decoration
H 17.2 cm – Inv. no. T 779
Red Polished Ware II–IV; purchased in
Cyprus about 1960
gift of Oskar Liebeck 1984

The biconical squat body of the jug is topped by a narrow cylindrical neck with a beaked spout. A vertical basket handle extends from the shoulder to the middle of the neck of this hand-made vessel. Vertical and horizontal suspension loops are attached axially along the neck, the beaked spout and the body. Delicate raised lines, some of them zigzag and diagonal, encircle the surface. The reddish-brown burnished coat and the lines in relief recalling the repoussé technique suggest metal prototypes in bronze or copper.

More or less bird-shaped vases were popular in all Aegean and Anatolian

civilisations. Suspension holes served to allow the vessels to be hung up in net-like holders and thus stabilised.

PG

Libation Vessel in the Form of a Bull

1550–1400 BC; Late Bronze Age
clay, painted, H 12 cm – Inv. no. T 592
Base Ring I Ware
Mühlmann/Seelig gift 1926

This hand-made rhyton, or vessel, is in the shape of a standing bull. The cylinder-shaped body has a filler neck in the nape of the animal's neck just in front of the bow-shaped strap handle. The funnel-shaped mouth forms the

opening of the spout. Eyes, ears, horns, legs and tail were modelled by hand. The matt, brown-black slip was originally painted with white bands. These small vases are common in Late Bronze Age tombs in Cyprus. The bull, being the biggest domestic cattle and sacrificial animal, provides an obvious model for the form of a libation vessel used for liquid offerings in cultic ceremonies.

PG

Greece
Early Late Stone Age,
4000–2500 BC

Idol

4000–3000 BC;
Middle to Late Neolithic
clay, incised decoration
H 8.3 cm – Inv. no. ALg 135
from Thespiai, Boeotia
on loan since 1973

This hollow fragment is part of a hand-made standing or seated idol that perhaps bore an attribute in its forearms crossed in front of its chest. The pale leather-coloured clay is an average of 5 mm thick. In the calotte of the skull is a round opening measuring ca 15 mm. The surface of the clay shows neat burnishing lines. The shoulders were attached separately, as indicated by the broken edge of the right one. The pronounced oval, disk-shaped face seems tilted up towards the sky. Very expressive are the highly abstract facial features: the ears and the nose with pricked holes, both pinched out of the clay mass, as well as the straight slit eyes with sculptural lids and eyebrows.

The expressive physiognomy and upward-turned disk-shaped faces widespread among the Middle to Late Neolithic idols from Boeotia and central Greece seem to live on as a typically Greek art form down to the figural Greek Geometric Period of the first millenium BC.   PG

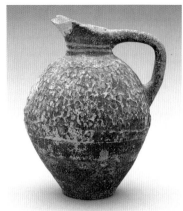

Greece
Bronze Age, 2500–1150 BC

Jug with Beaked Spout
2000–1850 BC; Middle Minoan
clay, painted, relief decoration
H 15.5 cm – Inv. no. T 799
MM I Kamares Ware;
purchased in Crete about 1960
gift of Oskar Liebeck 1984

The jug, with an ovoid body on a clay base, has a short neck with a beaked spout and a handle round in section extending from the shoulder to the edge of the lip. The body has thick walls, the clay diluted with sand and coated with a matt grey slip. Except for the cone-shaped lower body, neck and handle, the vase was covered before firing with thick clay slip in a textured technique known as Barbotine. The Barbotine zone is painted brown with small white dots and a few large red ones, and framed above and below by white and red bands. White hatching covers the handle. This widespread terracotta ware of the Middle Minoan period is named after one of its early find-places, the Kamares cave in southern Crete. The matt painting (light on dark) and the imitation of natural textures (shells, warts, scales, bark) are considered typical expressions of the natural and vegetal forms that Minoan art strove to represent. PG

Mistress of the Animals
1400–1300 BC; Late Minoan
gem, agate, W 3.03 cm – Inv. no. Ge 6
LM III A/B; from the Late Mycenaean tholos tomb of Menidi (suburb of Athens)
gift from the estate of H.G. Lolling 1899

In a special way, the motif is engraved into the lentoid (lense-shaped) precious stone, with a horizontal hole drilled through it so that several white layers of chalcedony form a striped

interpreted as snakes that she holds. The Mistress of Animals and the Snake Goddess are familiar subjects in Minoan art and testify to the religious attitude towards the power of the female divinity over the animal world. The motif in the form of a heraldic seal continues down to early Greek art.

PG

band in the agate (fortress or banded agate). In the middle of the scene stands a woman with uplifted arms and nude (?) upper body, her lower body dressed in a flounced skirt. On either side under her arms stands a lion facing outwards, its hindquarters hidden behind her skirt. This scene of a woman with lions depicts the divine 'goddess of the animals' (Greek: Potnia Theron). The curved lines rising diagonally outwards from either side of her waist have been interpreted from analogous scenes as abstract bull's horns. The curved lines with thickened ends above her head and arms are

Clay Larnax with Lid

1350–1300 BC; Late Minoan
clay, painted, L 99 cm – Inv. no. ALg 21
reported found in a tomb near Iráklion, Crete
on loan from the Peter and Irene Ludwig collection since 1975

The clay coffin or larnax in the form of a chest with a gabled lid on top stands on four feet, which are attached at the bases of reinforced corner posts. Vertical handles below the upper rim of the box correspond to eyelets on the edge of the lid, so that the lid and the box can be tied together. The box and the lid are assembled from clay panels before firing and smoothed out

along the joints and edges inside and out. The floor panel has holes in it along the centre and in the corners. These could have served both as firing holes during production or to speed up the decomposition of the body, buried in a crouching position with knees drawn up.

Painting the corner posts with checkerboard patterns, spiral foliage and circular segments emphasises the structure of the box, which is based on wooden prototypes. The sides are decorated with stylised plant motifs (blossoms, papyrus, nautilus) and a checkerboard band.

The majority of the larnakes in use since the Early Minoan Period has ornamental or floral decoration. Common types are the bathtub or oval shape and the rectangular chest with a gabled lid that is unique to Crete.

PG

Cup

octopus
1400–1300 BC; Late Mycenaean
clay, painted, H 19 cm – Inv. no. T 374
Late Helladic III A; from Attica (?)
purchased 1895

The long-stemmed drinking cup stands on a wide, slightly convex base plate. Two vertical ribbon handles

attached where the sides bulge out end on the edge of the lip. A large octopus seen from the front is painted in brownish black on both front and back of the cup. The large staring eyes as well as the suction cups along the body and the decoratively curved tentacles are painted with a pale slip. The freely moving marine creature covering the entire surface is based on Minoan art, but arranged symmetrically and related axially to the shape of the vessel in typically Mycenaean fashion.

PG

Clay Larnax

mourners, winged being
1300–1200 BC; Late Mycenaean
clay, painted, L 106.5 cm –
Inv. no. ALg 1
Late Helladic III B, found in a tomb near Tanagra, Boeotia
on loan from the Peter and Irene Ludwig Collection since 1964

Only the box on four cube-shaped feet has been preserved of this chest-shaped coffin (larnax). It is made of four clay panels joined before firing and smoothed out along the joints and edges. The floor panel is reinforced on the interior by four crosswise strips. The twelve irregularly distributed round holes in it are typical for the clay larnakes of this Mycenaean cemetery. They could both have served as firing holes during production or to ensure the rapid decomposition of the body, which was buried with its knees drawn up. The painted checkerboard decoration underscores the corner posts that are merely suggested by incised lines. The long sides are subdivided by a central checkerboard panel into two zones. They contain standing women in long gowns

with braids down to their waists: on side B their hands are clasped above their heads in the gesture of lamentation and their throats scratched bloody; on side A their raised hands tousle their wild hair. On one of the narrow sides hovers a female figure in long robes with braids down to her hips. She wears a flat head-dress topped with an S-shaped feather (?). Outspread raised wings replace her arms.

Burial in clay larnakes was limited in Mycenaean times to a few regions and persons. The particular importance of these images is that they demonstrate the appearance of the ritual lamentation documented in the Greek period on coffins as early as Mycenaean times. The interpretation of the winged being is still an open question: a Mycenaean goddess or the spirit of the deceased?   PG

Sword

1230–1150 BC; Late Mycenaean
bronze, cast, L 79.9 cm – Inv. no. Br 761;
Late Helladic III C; from Greece (?)
purchased 1998

Towards the end of the 13th century BC this type of sword suddenly became fashionable (heavy, long, slashing sword type known as Naue II) in Late Mycenaean civilisation. It had originated in central Europe. The long blade and the hilt – formerly with 'horns' projecting laterally – are cast in one piece. The grip and the pommel of wood or bone atop it would have been attached with rivets. The sword would have been carried in a sheath by a strap. This new type of weapon was presumably introduced to Greece through trade and immigration from the north. As an effective weapon of attack, this slashing type of sword rapidly spread in the Aegean area when manufactured locally. It replaced the swords common earlier and presumably proved its worth especially in the wars at the end of the Late Mycenaean realm. *PG*

Greece
Geometric Period
1000–700 BC

Jug with Lid
750–725 BC; Attic
clay, painted, H 52 cm – Inv. no. T 548
Late Geometric
purchased in Athens from the Lambros collection 1929

The early Iron Age revival in the Greek cultural environment after the end of the Bronze Age is called the Geometric Period. The term derives from the characteristic style of vase decoration at this time. This large jug has a wide strap handle, a body ribbed in low relief and a wide neck with a round mouth. The pronounced shapes and dense ornamentation exhibit the typical features of the rhythmical and textured formal structure of Geometric art. Besides the geometrical and abstract ornament there are some stylised figural elements, such as snakes, birds and flowers. These figural motifs could be related to the vase's use in sepulchral rituals as a cinerary urn, as grave-goods or as a monument on a tomb. The snake associated with the earth shelters the soul of the deceased; the bird, like the flower, is a symbol of life. *PG*

Horse
750–700 BC; Spartan
bronze, cast, H 7 cm – Inv. no. Br 616
Late Geometric
purchased in Athens
gift of F. Dümmler 1899

The long-legged horse stands on a platform decorated with cut-out triangles. A dowel projecting from the end used to support the tail. The horse's high neck with blade-bone and mane, its heavy thighs, and its hocks with their thorn-like projections are strongly emphasised. Its rod-shaped head with small ears and its thin, tubular body and stilt-like lower legs accent its slenderness. Physical volume and organic unity have been superseded in favour of

standardised individual parts of the body and a tension-filled silhouette. Stylistic details allow us to allocate the figure to Spartan Geometric art. PG

tor lies on its back. The old King of Troy points towards his slain son with outstretched arms and begs to redeem the body against ransom. The weapons and body of the Trojan leader had become the booty of the champion of the Greek besiegers of Troy. Side B: single combat between two heavily armed men (hoplites) over another fallen in battle, his armour the precious booty that lures the winner. Homer portrays the ransom of the body of Hector in a detailed and moving passage of the Iliad XXIV, 468ff. This vase painting is one of the rare early examples of the otherwise frequently depicted corpus of Trojan legends. The scene on B cannot be narrowed down to a specific single combat but refers indirectly to the story on side A and to battles in general. PG

Greece
Archaic Period
700–480 BC

The Ransom of Hector's Body
storage vase (amphora)
about 550 BC; Attic; Group E
clay, black-figured painting
H with lid 52 cm – Inv. no. T 674
purchased 1963

The bulging form gave the vase painter room for a large wide picture in the glossy clay technique with additional dark red and white as well as incised decoration. Side A: Achilles, reclining on a couch (kline), turns to face the white-haired King Priam and Briseis (?) behind him. Thrown on the floor under the kline and the adjacent dining table, the naked corpse of Hec-

Satyr Misusing an Amphora

drinking bowl. 520–500 BC; Attic

sign. by potter Panphaios; attrib. to
Nikosthenes painter

clay, red-figured painting

D to the outer edge 31 cm – Inv. no. ALg
214

on loan from the collection of Paul
Dierichs since 1977

The painting on this wide drinking
bowl (kylix) with a steeply rising rim
is limited to a masterly tondo painted
inside on the bottom. A satyr with a
horse's tail leans forward and thrusts
his erect penis into a pointed amphora
that he holds in front of himself with
both arms. He rests his massive head
on the vase as though listening and he
glances both mischievously and lustily
out of the corners of his eyes at the
vase. His face, seen frontally, with its
bulbous nose, thick lips, bushy eyebrows, low forehead and erect horse's
ears, is surrounded by thick curly hair
and a large pointed beard. Beginning
in front of his feet, running right to
left along the outline of the tondo, is a
dark red inscription naming the potter
PANPHAIOS EPOIESEN ("Pan-
phaios made it"). The same red slip is
used to paint the fine inner contours

and the burgundy red wreath around
the satyr's forehead.

The satyr, in the entourage of
Dionysos, being half human and half
horse personifies the untameable animal force of nature. Wine mixed with
water was served and passed around in
such bowls to guests at a drinking-
party (symposium). PG

Single Combat, Sirens, Lions

drinking cup. 575–550 BC;
Middle Corinthian

clay, black-figured painting

H 8.8 cm – Inv. no. S 1

attrib. to the Samos painter

1894 Samos excavation, W necropolis,
tomb 21

on loan since 1896; purchased 1998

Painted on the front (side A) of this
steep-sided cup (kotyle) in black-figured lustrous clay and with incised lines

is a scene of single combat flanked by two watching sirens. The two nude warriors, wearing helmets and greaves, attack each other with raised lances, holding their shields up to protect their left flanks and to shove the opponent. On the back (side B) two symmetrical lions stand opposite each other, turning around to look behind them, on either side of a lotus palmette ornament.

Heraldic-looking compositions with warriors in single combat, beasts of prey and fabulous creatures number among the most common motifs in Corinthian vase painting. Sirens can be understood as spirit birds, referring to the fateful outcome of the combat. Other vessels showing the same artist's hand and same technique can be attributed to the painter of this cup.

This vase belongs to the important archeological finds from the museum's excavation in 1894 in the archaic Greek necropolis of Samos. Parts of the minor objects were allowed to be transferred to Kassel.   PG

appeared at ritual celebrations on the street, in the theatre and in the sanctuary. They radiate animal joy and ecstasy.

This smaller than life-sized terracotta mask was found in a tomb containing another terracotta mask, terracotta figures, vessels, and a shell, suggesting that these grave-goods refer to the Dionysiac cult. The holes on either side recall the life-sized masks made of linen or leather, documented in art as well as preserved, tied on over the faces of actors and participants in rituals.   PG

Silenus Mask
550–500 BC; Eastern Greek, Samian
clay, painted, H 17.7 cm – Inv. no. S 52
1894 Samos excavation, W necropolis, tomb 48
on loan since 1896; purchased 1998

The face of this originally painted terracotta mask is framed by a wide pointed beard and cap-like hair. The slanted eyes, bushy eyebrows, bulbous nose with huge nostrils, thick lips and horse's ears turn the human face into a creature half man and half horse, a silenus or satyr. These hybrids accompanying the god Dionysos in myths

Two Jugs
550–500 BC; Samian or Carian
1894 Samos excavation, allegedly from Caria
clay, black-figured painting, sickle pattern
H 25.2 cm – Inv. nos. S 10, ALg 40
on loan since 1896; purchased 1998
on loan from the Paul Dierichs collection since 1974

The very advanced art of ornamentation in black-figured vase painting of the eastern Greek region is documented by these two jugs with an upward-curving handle and cloverleaf mouth (oinochoe). The painted eyes on the

Corinthian Helmet

about 490 BC; Eastern Greek, Carian
(?); allegedly from Caria
bronze, embossed
total H 40.5 cm – Inv. no. ALg 275
on loan from the Paul Dierichs collection
since 1980

rim and the sickle ornament that recalls feathers on the body suggest that
these vases could be seen as bird-
shaped. They thus belong to a cultural tradition going back to the early
Aegean Bronze Age.

To what extent find-places permit
conclusions about production sites has
long been discussed in archaeological
research. In the common regional
language of forms, the distinguishing
details, filiation and influences still
remain to be determined.   *PG*

This helmet should be regarded along
with several terracotta vessels of the
same provenance as grave-goods from
an eastern Greek Carian cemetery in
the region around Mylasa. Typologically,
its form relates to Corinthian helmets
in their final stage of development.
With its riveted sheetmetal in the shape
of bull's horns and ears, it must have
emphasised the special status of its
wearer. Bulls have played a major role
in Greek myths from ancient times
thanks to their size, strength, wildness
and tameability, e.g. myths about Zeus,
Europa, Dirke, Hercules, Theseus, Pasi-
phae. Moreover, oxen were the biggest,
strongest and most important domestic
cattle throughout antiquity.   *PG*

Zeus and Hermes

drinking bowl. 550–525 BC; Spartan
attrib. to the Chimaera painter
clay, black-figured painting
D 29.4 cm – Inv. no. T 354
purchased about 1895

The bowls handed around during a
ceremonial symposium bear images
from both mythology and the daily
life of the symposiasts. They illustrate
divine forces, are educational with
scenes of civic virtues or entertaining
with human and all-too-human stories. Athens and Sparta were the major
production centres of such drinking
bowls with masterly figural painting.
This black-figured one from Sparta
shows Zeus and Hermes in conversation on the inside of the bowl. The
father of the gods in a long gown,
enthroned on a chair (klismos) with
his feet resting on a stool, turns gestu-
ring towards the smaller messenger of
the gods standing before him. Hermes
in his travelling clothes, with winged
shoes and herald's staff, seems to be

listening attentively. Behind Zeus is
the eagle sacred to him; under the chair
is a rosette; under the line of the
ground is a pair of geese and a lotus
and ivory ornament. The outside of
the bowl is covered with ornamental
friezes of a string of buds, bands, a row
of sickles and monochrome zones. PG

Storage Jar

600–500 BC; Cretan; from Crete
clay, relief decoration, H 155 cm –
Inv. no. T 765
purchased 1982

Made by being built up in sections,
this thick vessel has the shape of a
pointed amphora with a wide mouth.
Protruding rings and stamped bands
encircle the body of the vase down to
its solid conical base. They recall
hoops or ropes that hold together bar-
rels made of wood or other organic
materials. Running along the shoulder
in front is a band of waves and griffons' heads facing left. Above it on the
neck stands a sphinx facing right and
flanked by two Ionic columns on cube-
shaped plinths. The sphinx with its
lion's body and feathered wings has

what is probably a woman's head with long incised hair down its neck; a budding branch sweeps back from the parting. The lion's tail curls upwards like a volute. At the attachment points of the handles on the neck, three-dimensional separately applied Gorgons' heads stare at the viewer.

Large clay storage jars (pithoi) for food (grain, oil, olives, wine) had been in use since the Bronze Age both in the magazines of centres of political power and for the producers' domestic supply. In the Greek Archaic period pithoi with relief decoration were manufactured mainly in Crete, Rhodes, the Cyclades and Boeotia.

Sphinxes, Gorgons and griffons function as guardians in Greek mythology and are here presumably to protect the vital contents from unauthorized users. *PG*

Iris, the Winged Messenger of the Gods (?)

altar, about 500 BC; Western Greek; from Sicily

clay, painted (?), H 54 cm – Inv. no. ALg 61
on loan from the Paul Dierichs collection since 1975

This clay altar (arula) consists of an upright rectangular box that is open at the bottom and inserted into a projecting plinth below and a similar slab forming a cover on top. Each of the short sides has two round holes suitable for the insertion of carrying rods to transport the altar. The two holes in the cover were presumably meant to allow liquid offerings (libations) to run through the hollow altar into the ground.

On the facade a girl shown in relief, her knees and arms bent in the Archaic scheme for running, hurries towards the right. Her speed and mobility are evident from the large

wings on her shoulders and her winged feet. Her frontal head with an Archaic smile wears a diadem; the hair on her forehead and shoulders is sculptural. Her frontal upper body is dressed in clothing gathered at the waist; her lower body, seen from the side, in a skirt with a stepped bunch of folds. Whether the figure was originally painted no longer shows.

The use of portable clay altars in domestic rites, in the sanctuary and in sepulchral rituals is documented mainly for Greek settlements on the south coast of Sicily. The closest parallels are found in Gela and Selinunt. Whether the winged girl represents Iris, the divine messenger between immortals and humans, and the goddess of the rainbow, remains mere speculation for the time being.   PG

Pegasus

650–600 BC; Insular Greek
gem, steatite
D 2.5 cm – Inv. no. Ge 16
gift of F. Dümmler 1899

Found in an Early Archaic tomb in the Trypiti cemetery in Melos, this gem with a round composition is technically simple but artistically compelling. The winged horse facing left jumps over a snake with a wide-open mouth. Its forelegs are shown in the running position with bent knees typical of the period. Of its hind legs, only the one closest to the viewer is visible. A ball appears between its mane and feathered wing.

In Greek mythology Pegasus was born of Poseidon, the god of the sea and shaker of the earth. To this parentage Pegasus owes his body of

a horse as well as this snake. The ball, perhaps a star, could refer to the air (ether) governed by Pegasus or to his being carried off to become a constellation.   PG

Greece

Classical Period
480–330 BC

The Kassel Apollo

Roman copy about 100 AD of a Greek original about 450 BC
attrib. to Phidias
marble, H of the figure 200 cm – Inv. no. Sk 3
purchased in Rome 1777

This statue has been one of the major works of ancient art in Kassel since 1777. It is the most complete ancient marble copy of this statue of the god, and comes from a Roman villa of the imperial period near Sabaudia south of Rome. Apollo, with long curly hair on his forehead and down to his shoulders, is standing nude in contrapposto. His head slightly bent, he looks past the curve of his extended left hand into the distance. In his other

of justice and of light appears unapproachable at the same time. *PG*

Grave Stele of Aristodika

about 350 BC; from Crete
marble, H 86.5 cm – Inv. no. ALg 243
on loan from the Paul Dierichs collection
since 1978

The custom of erecting sculpted steles in memory of the dead has been documented since Mycenaean times. In classical Athens it became a widespread middle-class convention and led to burgeoning representation that was repeatedly restricted by decree.

Dating from the 4th century BC, this relief with three figures in a shrine-like tombstone (naiskos) is inscribed with their names. A woman named Aristodika seated on the right and her husband Akesidamos standing before her are looking at each other and holding each other's right hand. Between them in the background appears their son (?) Sotadas. Their

hand he presumably held a laurel wreath. A total of 27 ancient copies dating from Roman times and preserved as fragments replicate this statue, and it is depicted on some ancient coins and gems. On the basis of what the copies indicate, the lost original is thought to be a 2-metre high bronze of the Greek Classical Period around 450 BC. It has long been speculated that the bronze statue mentioned by the travel writer Pausanias (about 170 AD) of Apollo Parnopios (locust killer) by the sculptor Phidias on the Acropolis of Athens can be identified with the Kassel type. This figure embodies the new Classical Greek image of Apollo: youthful vigour, concentrating inwardly on the movements of standing and stepping, ready for action with long-distance weapons, and with the laurel that has purifying, healing power. Proud, while turning slightly to face a mortal, the god of the oracle,

holding hands can be interpreted either as a scene from everyday life, or as the farewell to the enthroned departed, and as the meeting in the afterlife between the newly deceased man and his predeceased wife. What probably mattered most to the viewer in ancient times was having a visual memorial to relatives and ancestors on the cemetery near the settlement.

The names in Doric dialect and the documented provenance of this stele from the south coast of Crete indicate that this art form developed in Athens was adopted in almost all Greek regions during the Classical Period.   PG

A Warrior's Farewell

krater, about 470 BC; Attic
attrib. to the Harrow painter
clay, red-figured painting
H 43 cm – Inv. no. T 716
gift of the Investitions- und Handelsbank Frankfurt 1969

At a symposium, wine and water would be mixed in a krater and chilled. The pictures on these ceremonial vases are quite likely to reflect educational ideals and middle-class virtues. In the centre on side A stands a young warrior with long curly hair, armed with a pushed up helmet, shield with a snake emblem, greaves and upright lance. His cloak suggests that he is about to set out. He turns towards a woman on the far left. She hands him a ribbed libation dish (phiale) that she has filled from a jug in her other hand. On the far right, facing in the same direction as the warrior, stands a bearded man with a gnarled stick. The trio depicts the family farewell ceremony for a son going to battle. On principle, it was the mother who per-

formed the farewell sacrifice. The scene visualises the fulfilment of duty and readiness to make sacrifices of the middle-class family in the Classical polis of Athens. On the back (side B) young men wearing cloaks converse in a palaestra (?). A relationship to the scene on the front may be intended. Nevertheless, this motif soon became a shallow, long-lived, stereotype decorative scheme.   PG

Parodies of Myths

drinking cup, about 420 BC, Boeotian
workshop of the Kabir painter
clay, black-figured painting
H 20.5 cm – Inv. no. ALg 18
on loan from the collection of Peter and Irene Ludwig since 1968

In the rural sanctuary of Kabir near Thebes, mysteries were celebrated with burlesque performances (comedies, farces). Oversized drinking cups painted in the old-fashioned black-figured technique during the high Classical Period are characteristic for this cult site in Boeotia.

Both sides of this drinking cup (Kabir skyphos) show scenes with groups of figures under heavy grape-

vine garlands. On the front (side A) a nude, ithyphallic, bearded man with a helmet and drawn sword threatens a woman seeking shelter near a pillar-like idol of Athena on a stepped pediment on the far left of the picture. On the right a woman runs towards a nude, helmeted, beardless man, who threatens her with his raised sword while she turns away – perhaps she, too, is running towards a pillar-like idol on the far right. Both grotesquely drawn groups of figures caricature dramatic Trojan legends. On the left the Greek hero Ajax is chasing the Trojan king's daughter, the prophetess Cassandra, who flees from rape in vain to the asylum of the altar. On the right Menelaos is threatening his regained but disinterested wife Helen.

On the back (side B) a flautist strikes up for a dance on the left to a nude man with bound feet. On the right a Negroid nude man holds a glowing torch in the face of an old man dragging a rock bound to his foot. Parody, irony, travesty, making fun of the gods, the myths and historical personages were part of the Classical Greek theatre and of this orgiastic Dionysiac mystery cult. *PG*

Water Jug

500–400 BC

bronze, embossed and cast

H 39.2 cm – Inv. no. Br 734

purchased 1987

The three-handled type of water jug was used for over 800 years in Greek and Roman antiquity. From the 7th century BC to 2nd century AD the work of carrying fresh water home from the well was usually done by girls, balancing the jugs on their heads.

The body of the vase consists of thin sheetmetal, the handles and the base are cast. The basket handles have leaf-shaped attachment points soldered and riveted onto the sides of the vase. Bronze vessels were very highly valued in ancient times because of their durability and light weight. They turn up less frequently in excavations than terracotta vessels because they had already been used repeatedly in antiquity and the metal was subject to corrosion in the soil. This vase ranks among a Classical type named after a presumed centre of production in Chalkis. *PG*

Athena (O) – Owl (R)

2 tetradrachmas; about 420 BC;
Attic
silver; weight 17.14 g, 17.18 g
Inv. nos. Mü 13 (O), Mü 661 (R)
gift of the Stadtsparkasse Kassel 1984
(Mü 13); purchased 1998 (Mü 661)

Stamped on the head, or obverse, of coins minted in Athens since the 6th century BC was the head of the city's goddess in profile, wearing a helmet with an olive wreath and a spiralling vine around its edge. The helmet exposes her charming face, hair and earring. On the reverse, indented by a square die, stands an owl (little owlet, Athene noctua) turning right, its head frontal. The abbreviation AΘE identifies the Athens mint. The crescent of the moon probably refers to the fact that the owl sacred to the goddess is particularly vigilant and active at night. The olive branch, like that on the helmet on the obverse, refers to the economic wealth that the polis owes to this plant sacred to Athena.

The Greek word drachma is the original term for "what you can hold in one hand," namely, 6 spears (oboloi) = pre-monetary currency in the form of iron implements. It was issued in 1, 2, 3, 4, 10 and 12-drachma coins and subdivided into 1–6 oboli and other denominations.

Corresponding to their political structure, autonomous Greek city-states (poleis) stamped coins of their own with distinctive coats of arms guaranteeing the weight and standard. In Classical times a tetradrachmon was worth a week's wages or a bushel of wheat (ca. 50l).   PG

Griffon

bezel of a ring; about 400 BC;
Eastern Greek
agate, W 2.19 cm – Inv. no. Ge 23
purchased before 1776

The shape of this fortress or banded agate recalls a scarab (beetle-shaped gem). It was mounted on a metal ring piercing through it, now lost. The engraving shows a griffon jumping towards the left and framed by a line. These fabulous creatures with an eagle's head, wings, and a lion's body were honoured in Greek times as protecting spirits and guardians. Legend has it that they guarded the gold in the land of the Hyperboreans "on the edges of the inhabited world," paradisiacal fields where Apollo lived in wintertime and that he promised to his followers. They were also called the "dogs of

Zeus." Familiar to the Greeks since Minoan and Mycenaean times, they had been taken over from Near Eastern civilisations, where they stood for divine power, temporal majesty, and served as guardians of tombs and gates. This gem made by a Classical eastern Greek workshop is stylistically related to Achaemenid, Graeco-Persian hunting scenes. *PG*

Paris and Helen

storage jar; about 350 BC;
Apulian
attrib. to the Laodameia painter
clay, red-figured painting
H 48.3 cm – Inv. no. T 723
purchased 1971

This pear-shaped large vase (pelike) is painted with red-figured courtship scenes typical for late Classical pottery grave-goods in Western Greece. On side A, Paris lounges on a throne wearing Oriental costume, his sceptre beside him, feet on a stool. He looks over to Helen, who turns towards him. She touches her hair and gathers up the side of her gown. A woman behind her has brought a basket (kalathos). Aphrodite stands on the left beside Paris. Elaborately dressed and ornamented, she extends towards the couple a sacrificial bowl that she has

filled from a libation jug in her other hand. Drifting down from above under a lyre, Eros crowns Paris with a wreath. In the background on either side of Eros a woman with a mirror and xylophone is seated on the right and another with a tambourine on a box on the left. At Paris's feet lies a swan, the animal sacred to the goddess of love. On the back (side B) is a similar but more general scene: a young man and girl with cupids and female companions.

According to legend, Aphrodite and Eros made the fateful match between the Trojan prince when he was a guest at the court of the Greek King of Sparta and his wife Helen. The other figures and implements refer to the marriage ceremony. Late Classical vase painting features colourful scenes with many figures in an 'airy' perspective. *PG*

Greece

Hellenistic Period
330–30BC

Askos with Figures

about 280 BC; Apulian, Canosian
clay, relief and figures moulded and
attached separately,
polychrome painting,
H 81.5 cm – Inv. no. T 970
purchased 1992

The shape of the vessel with a globular body, bow handle and spout is derived from that of a wineskin (askos)
made of leather. It is made of soft,
fired clay painted with water-soluble
paints on a white slip. It can therefore
only have been used as grave-goods.

Above the small flat base a large
head of Medusa or a Gorgon decor-
ates the front of the flask. The beautiful face of the female demon, fending
off evil while usually spreading fear
and horror, is surrounded by decoratively wavy hair intertwined with
snakes tied together in a knot under
her chin. Emerging from the globular
flask on either side, at shoulder
height, are two gesticulating centaurs
pointing diagonally upwards and for-
wards, and at mid-level, two horses.
These attached front halves of fabulous creatures and animals have
sculptural details, such as the cape
fluttering upward from the nape of
the centaur's neck. On a podium opposite the spout stands a girl in a pink
and blue gown, her gaze upturned
and arms raised in prayer.

Polychrome vases with a light slip
and separately attached three-dimensional figures are typical grave-goods
of the early Hellenistic period in Sicily (Centuripe) and northern Apulia

(Canosa). Whether this type of vessel
and its sculptural ornament are related to concepts of the hereafter in
the Aphrodisiac-female or the Dionys-
iac-male domain is still under discussion in research.   *PG*

Lion

about 300 BC; from Tarento (?)
limestone (pietra tenera)
L 118 cm – Inv. no. ALg 5
on loan from the Peter and Irene Ludwig
collection since 1968

In a crouching tense position, the lion
turns his head sideways and slightly
upwards. His forelegs are almost parallel, hind legs taking a step. Excited, he
exposes his teeth in a slightly open
mouth, the upper lip curled, chops
drawn back. Deep-set eyes pop out
from under heavy brows. Short fleshy
ears emerge from his dense shaggy
mane. Short tufts of hair stand out like
spines from his legs. His tail with its
tassel presumably reached down to the
ground between his two hind paws.
The serrated surface is made to suggest the texture of short fur.

The lion probably comes from a tombstone, where he was seen both as a guardian and a life-destroying thief. Stylistically attributed to the period from Late Classical to early Hellenistic, the sculpture is one of the rare, impressive animal figures of the art of Magna Graecia in Tarento. PG

Berenice II

246–222 or 221 BC; Ptolemaic

from Alexandria (?)

marble, painted, H 38 cm –

Inv. no. Sk 115

purchased 1961

The larger than life-sized portrait shows a mature woman with a distinctive physiognomy: a full, wide face with a dimple on her chin, a small mouth with a slightly drooping, full lower lip below a very curvilinear upper one, a low forehead, and low set-back ears. The corners of her mouth, deeply indented with a drill and made to droop, give her whole face a slightly melancholy expression. Her slightly

wavy hair is parted in the middle and pulled back. A diadem, visible particularly on the left side, characterises the woman as a monarch.

Despite a certain idealisation, the close resemblance of this head to portraits on coins indicates that this sculpture portrays Berenice II, the wife of the Ptolemaic king, Ptolemaios III. Broken off at the top of the neck, it is likely to have topped a statue about 3.5 m high, painted in colour and presumably dressed in a

chiton and himation, which probably stood with a statue of her husband in a cult shrine in Alexandria. The dowel hole in the calotte could be from a crown of Isis, because the wife of the Pharaoh was often identified with the goddess Isis. Other attributes, such as a sceptre and double cornucopia, would have referred to the blessings bestowed on Egypt by the reign of the Ptolemies.

The queen, who was already worshipped ritually during her lifetime and was frequently identified with the goddess Isis, came from Cyrene, where she herself reigned. In 221 BC she was murdered by her son. Presumably she had wanted to share his rule. *MK*

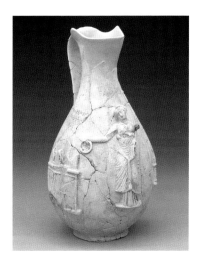

Berenice II Performing a Sacrifice

jug

246–221 BC; Ptolemaic

found in Lasaia, Crete (?)

silica ceram, relief decoration;

inscriptions; fragments of blue glaze,

H 29.5 cm – Inv. no. T 1018

purchased 1996

This hand-made jug (oinochoe) with a cloverleaf-shaped mouth is made of a quartzose mass, so-called 'Egyptian faience'. Because of the unusual properties of this material, the formulas and the manufacturing process for siliceous ceramic artefacts having been developed since the early Bronze Age, it originally had a blue glazed surface. In a few places fragments of this glaze, which is not resistant to corrosion, have been preserved.

The strap handle, ribbed lengthwise, has a mask of silenus decorating its lower attachment point. On the body and shoulder zone a separately attached relief shows a woman dressed in a chiton and mantle beside a slim, conical, ritual column (baitylos) decorated with garlands and festoons. She carries a cornucopia in her left hand while performing a sacrifice with her right. The altar, depicted in perspective, has an inscription that reads: THEON EUERGETON ("to the benevolent gods"). The Greek inscription BERENIKES BASILISSES AGATHES TYCHES ("to Queen Berenice, the Agatha Tyche") identifies the woman as both Queen Berenice II and her own tutelary goddess at the same time. According to ancient Egyptian tradition, the deified queen who reigned with Pharaoh Ptolemaios III from 246 to 221 BC is here shown performing a sacrifice during the ritual celebrating her own cult. This type of jug, presumably used only for the cult of a monarch in the extended sphere of Ptolemaic influence, documents that traditional religious ideas continued to flourish during the Hellenistic period. *MK*

Oak Wreath Diadem

300–200 BC
gold, bronze, D 18 cm – Inv. no. V 63
purchased 1935

This diadem consists of a bronze
coronet covered with thin sheet gold
onto which oak leaves pointing towards the centre are attached in a
symmetrical arrangement. The centre
probably originally featured a rosette
or similar ornament perhaps made of
other materials and now lost. The oak
leaves were cut out of thin sheet gold.
The serrated edges and ribs in relief
on the surface of the leaves make
them look very naturalistic. About 3
cm apart, four groups of three leaves
each are attached on either side of
the bronze ring with their stems
twisted together as though knotted.

In all periods, gods as well as certain higher levels of society had the
privilege of wearing diadems. Wreaths
made of extremely thin sheet gold
were common in sepulchral ritual.
The Kassel wreath made of very
strong material is therefore unique.

Its owner probably wore it during his
lifetime for ritual celebrations or festivities before it was deposited in his
grave with him.   *MK*

Muse with a Large Cithara

Roman copy about 160 AD of a
Greek original about 150 BC
attrib. to Philiskos
marble, H 143 cm – Inv. no. ALg 81
on loan from the Paul Dierichs collection
since 1979

Seated on a rock, the muse wears a
short-sleeved chiton buttoned on her
shoulder and belted under her breast.
She has draped her mantle around her
lower body and legs. Her sandals are
attached with two straps passing between the big and second toes into
the sole. Her middle-parted hair is
combed softly away from her face and
loosely knotted at the nape of her
neck. The back of her head is covered
with a hood-like scarf that ends in a
sharp edge in the middle of her head.
Fragments of red paint have been

towards the right seems somewhat tense. It creates the impression that she has interrupted her playing only for a moment and is about to get up and continue. The only slightly finished back suggests that the figure is intended to be seen from the front. This sculpture is a copy made in the 2nd century of a Greek original dating from the 2nd century BC. Such works testify to the exemplary status of Greek civilisation and the high esteem in which it was held by the wealthy members of the population in Roman times.   *MK*

preserved on the hair at her temples. Her left arm holds a large cithara, commonly called a lyre, a stringed instrument of which only fragments of the sounding board remain on her left thigh and of the top of the frame (puntello) on her left shoulder. Her right hand, which probably held a plectrum for playing the strings, rests lightly on her right thigh.

The muse's emphatic upright posture with her torso turning slightly

Love scenes

drinking cup; about 100 BC;
Pergamum
clay, relief decoration, H 14.2 cm –
Inv. no. T 823
purchased 1987

This kantharos with relief decoration coated with black engobe (slip) has an almost cylindrical shape, slightly tapering upwards to the outsplayed rim. The sides taper sharply towards the conical base, set off from the body by a rim and ridges. The two strap handles on either side are reinforced

with clay caps on the top. Two appliqués showing scenes of love-making are attached on each side as decoration.

Vessels with images in relief had been popular since Classical times. The moulded appliqués allow different vessels to be produced in series.

The skyphos was one of the articles made in Pergamum since the 2nd century BC and exported to the entire Mediterranean region. Both the manufacturing process (the use of moulds) and the primarily erotic scenes (symplegmata) made this kind of relief ware the prototype for various kinds of Roman pottery.   *MK*

Italy
Villanova, Etruria
900–200 BC

Urn with a Bowl Cover
775–700 BC
Plain Style, Villanova Ic–II
impasto clay, burnished, incised
ornamentation
total H 49.5 cm – Inv. nos. T 1 and T 4
purchased about 1777

This slender biconical vessel without a base ring bulges out strongly in the middle of the body. The neck, tapering above a distinct groove, ends in a flaring rim. One handle protrudes horizontally between the body and the shoulder.

The incised geometric patterns formerly encrusted with white thus contrasted markedly with the glossy surface of the urn. The nested forms, swastika-shaped motifs, bands filled with diagonal lines or dots, and broad bands with alternating diagonally hatched or dotted meanders are characteristic motifs. The bowl used as a cover, also with one handle and with two knobs serving as grips on opposite sides, has a high conical base also without a base ring. Its geometrical ornament resembles that on the urn.

The hand-made pottery named after the proto-Etruscan site of Villanova near Bologna acquired its black metallic sheen from the very chalky, coarse clay and special firing technique used.

Biconical vessels of this kind, found covered with bowls in women's burial sites and covered with bronze or clay helmets in men's, are typical cinerary urns of the Villanova period. Used for burials, they evidently had only one handle for ritual reasons. Other handles were purposely broken off before a vessel was used as an urn.   *MK*

in between and a double ring above and below. The octagonal facetting of the shaft below the rings on the socket corresponds to that of socket of the blade. The rings may have served to secure a wire with which to attach the lance head to the wooden shaft.

The sword with the hilt and blade in one unit has a pommel shaped like a mushroom and a point like a carp's tongue. Its shape is typical for central Italy. The box shaped edge of the grip held inlaid organic material such as ivory or wood (now lost).   *MK*

Sword and Lance
800–600 BC; early Iron Age
middle Italic; grave-goods (?)
bronze, cast, L sword 46 cm; L lance blade
45 cm; L lance tip 51.5 cm – Inv. nos.
Br 762, 763 a. b.
purchased 1980

An ensemble rarely found together is a lance head with a lance bucket. The blade of this lance exhibits the typical willow leaf shape with a slightly rounded end. A protruding central rib extends from the shaft to the end. Octagonal on the outside, the socket of the blade is of round section inside. The facets end on the central rib. In the socket there are still the remains of an (ancient?) wooden shaft.

The lance head tapers to a conical point with a casting burr (?), and is of polygonal section. Its upper end is drilled through horizontally to attach the (lost) wooden shaft. The socket of the round lance head widens slightly at the edge. It is encircled with a series of embossed rings with four grooves

Fabulous Creatures and Warriors
Jug; 525–500 BC; Etruscan
bucchero clay, relief decoration,
H 25.4 cm – Inv. no. T 654
purchased 1947

Above a narrow, deeply profiled base ring, this jug (oinochoe) made of bur-

nished blackish-grey bucchero clay swells out to form an ovoid body. The almost horizontal shoulder tapers to a constricted neck ending in a cloverleaf spout. The strap handle curves from the rim to the shoulder.

The appliqué decoration on the vase imitates the very highly developed toreutics (metalworking techniques) in Etruria. The handle is decorated with a bearded warrior with a helmet, breastplate and lance, striding towards the right. Two ornamental friezes en-circle the vase. The one on the shoul-der features a winged chimaera (with a panther's head and on her back a goat's head) facing right, alternating with a bifoliate palmette; the one on the body shows a sphinx facing a seahorse. The friezes are bordered with two – and three-ribbed outer bands, respectively. Between them is a band with two outer rings and an incised wavy line along the middle of it. The same band also encircles the neck.

Where the handle meets the rim, two clay plaques in relief show two horse's heads back to back and a pomegranate.   MK

Man Performing a Sacrifice
200–100 BC; Etruscan
bronze, cast; eyes inlaid with red stones,
H 32 cm – Inv. no. Br 52
purchased in Rome 1777

The slim young man wears his mantle over his left shoulder across his back and hips, its end draped over his left arm. The tightly clinging fabric ex-poses the contours of his back and free leg, forming many parallel folds across front of his body. His narrow face with a high forehead and long nose has eyes inlaid with red stones. His hair, radiating from the back of his head, is long down his neck and forms short wisps around his face. According to similar examples, a sacrificial bowl would have been in his raised right hand and an incense vessel in his lowered left. A further reference to a sacrificial ceremony is the wreath of pointy protruding leaves the man wears on his head. Small bronze fig-ures of Etruscan provenance of this kind, most of them probably votive offerings in sanctuaries, are strongly influenced both iconographically and stylistically by Greek art. The relatively unfinished back of the statue suggests that it was mainly intended to be seen from the front.   MK

Girl

300–200 BC Etruscan

clay, H 149.5 cm – Inv. no. ALg 6

on loan from the Peter and Irene Ludwig collection since 1968

The girl wears a chiton evidently made of fine material, forming the typical V-shaped neckline fold standing slightly away from the neck and back. Gathered up in a belt under her breast, the gown falls in many intricate folds. Over it, a mantle forming only a few heavy folds, is draped over her left arm hanging in many folds down to the ground. The girl is holding the hem of her mantle in her right hand at her waist.

While the front view shows the folds of the mantle in detail, the back only shows the thicker hems of the cloak summarily. Her sandal-like shoes, evidently tied at the instep, are

elaborately decorated. Around her neck is a torque terminating in animal heads. The girl's hair is pulled back towards the back of her head in a knot that is now lost. A loose knot on her forehead is meant to prevent hair from falling in her face and distracting her.

The charming statuette belongs to the Etruscan cultural complex. This explains some of the hand-made figure's peculiarities, such as the somewhat inaccurate proportions. As directly comparable figures have not been preserved, its interpretation remains difficult. It probably shows an upper-class girl assisting at a ritual sacrifice. The lost attribute in her left hand may have been a sacrificial dish or jug.   *MK*

The Dioscurides, Helen, Leda

Mirror; 300–150 BC; Etruscan

found in Praeneste (?)

bronze, cast, incised decoration

L 23 cm – Inv. no. Br 755

purchased 1994

The hand mirror comprises a disk and a handle. The slightly convex front of the disk, with a grooved edge and fine row of beading around it, was originally polished as smooth as glass. It is attached to the handle by a segment along the edge inserted into a trilobe ribbed acanthus. Below this the handle is topped with a volute capital. It ends in the flat head of a deer. The concave back of the disk is surrounded by a raised flat frame and an angular raised edge with a ridge. On the back, the disk looks attached to the upper end of the handle.

A group of four figures framed all around with a laurel branch is en-

Imperium Romanum
Early Roman Empire
30 BC–100 AD

Agrippina Minor
about 60 AD
marble, H 29 cm – Inv. no. Sk 105
purchased 1928

The head of the Roman Empress Agrippina Minor (15–59 AD) seems to depict the facial features of the empress quite realistically. The differently positioned eyes and the deep folds encircling her throat in parallel lines are probably distinctive physiognomic details. Typical for the portrait of the empress (type IV) is also the hairdo of small, snail-like, tightly wound curls surrounding her face almost like a wig.

The head was meant to be inserted into a separately made statue. The joint would have been covered up by the paint colouring the whole statue.

Agrippina Minor, the wife of Emperor Claudius who reigned 41–54 AD, came from Cologne. After her marriage to Claudius she furthered the development of her native town

graved on the rounded form with a fine cutting tool. The two Dioscurides sit facing each other in the outer foreground. Only their lower bodies are dressed and they are characterised by their Phrygian caps, laced boots and the lances in their hands. Between them in the centre two women in long gowns stand in the background, presumably their sister Helen on the left and their mother Leda wearing a radiating diadem on the right.

In this late phase of Etruscan art, the move away from Greek and Hellenistic influence becomes increasingly evident. This also led to the adoption of home-grown themes. Nevertheless, the subjects of drawings on Etruscan mirrors usually continue to be drawn from Greek mythology and are often thought to be based on works of art in other genres.   PG

very generously, such as by conferring the status of a city upon it. She aided the accession of Nero, her son by her first marriage, to the imperial throne by murdering Claudius.   MK

Storage Jar
1–100 AD; from Asia Minor
clay, relief decoration, glazed
H 34.5 cm – Inv. no. T 709
purchased 1967

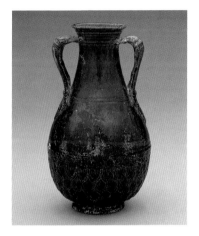

This pear-shaped amphora tapers gracefully upwards to the narrow neck, which ends in a rim encircled by multiple ridges. Starting below the rim, two ribbon handles end on the shoulder in foliate attachment points. Two sets of two encircling ridges divide the body of the vase into three almost equally high sections. The bottom section, with scaly ornament and a rosette frieze along the top, was made in a mould. The wheel-made upper section was added on the potter's wheel later. The separately made base was also attached in a further step.

After the first firing, it was fired second time, giving the beige clay vessel a yellowish brown inside and a dark to light green glaze outside. Both the coloured slip and individual features, such as the handle attachments on which separately formed rivet heads appear, imitate extremely popular but very expensive bronze vessels. Most people who bought pottery of this kind belonged to the less well-to-do levels of society, whose lifestyle and taste were nevertheless oriented on the luxury of the rich.   MK

One-Handled Cup and Saucer
50–100 AD
glass, total H 14.5 cm – Inv. nos. G 92 a. b.
purchased about 1900

This set consisting of a cup with one handle and a saucer was free-blown. The saucer with a steeply rising edge shows the typical pontilmark of this glassblowing technique underneath. From a pushed-in base ring, it flares upwards diagonally and ends in a plain, folded over, upright rim.

The cup shaped body of the drinking vessel also has a pushed-in base forming a hollow base ring. Above the shoulder, which is folded double to form a flange around its edge, and the constricted neck, is a plain outsplayed rim. The handle, curving out and down from below the flange, runs out in a wavy tail down the body.

In Roman times, glass dishes numbered among the luxury items that only the wealthy upper classes could afford. This also explains why some glasses and glass vessels show signs of repair.   *MK*

Dionysos and Ariadne (?)
about 50 AD; from Ostia
two-headed herm, formerly atop
a pillar-like shaft
marble, H 26 cm Inv. no. Sk 120
purchased 1964

The head of Dionysos-Bacchus (or Hermes-Mercury) is relatively undetailed and hence seems very Archaic. The face, in which only the cheekbones protrude strongly, is framed by a double row of staggered corkscrew curls divided from the hair on the head by a headband. The side view reveals two braids, one behind each ear. The full beard, side-whiskers and moustache are also depicted in the form of corkscrew curls.

The smile of Ariadne (or Dionysos-Bacchus), suggested by the slightly upward curved corners of her mouth, is also an archaising motif. The hair is parted down the middle and combed back in parallel waves held down by a ribbon and ends in two braids on either side of the head.

In Roman times, herms were set up along the roadside or in the open countryside, in the manner of today's wayside crosses and saints' shrines. They were also a popular form of decoration in large patrician homes. This herm from Ostia probably stood in the atrium or the entrance area of a large Roman villa.   *MK*

Young Mars Dancing
1–100 AD
bronze, cast, H 10.5 cm – Inv. no. Br 20
purchased before 1791

The Roman god of war is shown in a youthful athletic form. Mars wears his short mantle loosely draped in many

Athlete's Toiletries

bowl, 2 ointment jars,
2 strigils
1–100 AD; from Madytos
grave-goods (?)
bronze, cast
L of the bowl with handle 43 cm;
ointment jars H 9cm; L of the strigils
22.5 and 21 cm – Inv. nos. 638 (bowl);
Br 639 a. b. (ointment jars); Br 654. 655
(strigils)
purchased before 1912

The cast bronze bowl with delicate moulding around the outer edge is decorated with an elaborately ornamented handle. Two strands, surrounded by long sepals, profiled and held together in the centre by a silver-plated beaded string, end in dog's heads under a palmette. On the edge of the bowl a Gorgon's head, its silver-plated eyes effectively accented, is flanked by two dolphin's heads with ribbed unidentifiable objects in their mouths.

The two ointment jars bulge out to the shoulder from a small base. Above the very narrow neck, set off by a fine raised line, the lip of the funnel-shaped spout is emphasised by two protruding rings with a groove in between.

The two strap-shaped strigils (scrapers) have a wide, slightly concave, curved, bronze band bending at a right angle to the flattened handle.

This ensemble, possibly from a tomb, is an athlete's set of toiletry articles. The two ointment jars, their narrow openings allowing the precious contents to pour out only a drop at a time, contained the oil that athletes spread on their bodies before competitions. The excess oil was scraped off afterwards with a strigil.

folds around his hips and swinging back behind him. He has pushed up his helmet. His short frizzy curls protrude out from under it. In his outstretched left hand there should have been an upright tropaeum (trophy) while his right holds what is a partially preserved lance.

Representations of Mars of this type are typical for the Augustian period, when the concept of the revenging god of war (Mars Ultor) was replaced by that of a universally reigning Pax Romana. The Roman people had not only brought about this 'Roman peace' but also guaranteed its continuance. The form of the body in imitation of the Classical style and the slightly dancing stance recalling the dances performed by priests during rituals, correspond to the taste of the period around 100 BC when this motif was developed. Small statues of this kind depicting various gods were either erected in a Roman domestic shrine (lararium) or offered to a temple as votive gifts.   *MK*

The bowls served to scoop up water, with which the athletes rinsed off the sweat and dust of the arena and refreshed themselves. *MK*

Imperium Romanum
Middle Roman Empire
100–200 AD

Lucius Verus
(reigning Roman emperor)
161–169 AD
marble, H 65 cm – Inv. no. Sk 119
purchased in Rome 1963

This portrait bust shows a middle-aged man dressed in a tunic. The military commander's cloak draped over it in multiple folds is pinned together on his right shoulder with a round brooch. His short, thick, curly hair falls down low onto his forehead. The long hair of his beard looks similarly restless. Under his straight horizontal eyebrows, the pupils (hollowed out with a drill) are almost piercing.

Lucius Verus began his joint rule with Marcus Aurelius in 161 AD. His portrait is well known from coins. The suberb Kassel bust shows the official portrait type introduced upon the ruler's accession to the throne which, despite all idealisation, shows identifiable characteristic features. In addition, certain motifs, such as the lively hair and the drilled pupils, are marks of 2nd-century style. *MK*

Victoria

about 150 AD;
from Fossombrone
(Forum Sempronii)
bronze, cast; silver inlays
H 63.5 cm – Inv. no. Br 121
purchased 1777 in Rome

Victoria, the goddess of victory,
comes floating down, landing with
her left foot on a – probably correctly
restored – globe. Her raised hands
may have held a (victor's) wreath. The
goddess wears a peplum open at the
side and with many folds, its overhan-
ging part belted under her breast. The
belt and the shoulder fastenings of
the peplum are accented in silver. The
wind is flattening her gown against
her body and puffing out the hem
and the overhang in deeply recessed
folds. The goddess's youthful, serious
looking face is framed by middle-
parted hair gathered at the nape of
her neck and swept up over a headband. Her silver inlaid eyes are
lacking the pupils made of some
other material. On her huge wings
the plumage and especially the flight
feathers have been very carefully
chased. The slightly asymmetrical
position of the arms makes the figure
look very animated. The solid cast
statue is of excellent quality, which
speaks for the highly developed art of
bronzes of the mid-2nd century AD.

MK

Bowl

100–300 AD; terra sigillata
Rheinzabern style;
found in Leihgestern near Giessen
clay, relief, engobe
H 12.6 cm – Inv. no. T 641
purchased 1932

The sides of this bowl covered with
reddish-brown engobe show two
superimposed rows of animals jumping right – or leftwards: horses, deer
chased by hounds, hares and a peacock. A few stylised blossoms are also
scattered in this register, which is bordered above by an egg and dart frieze
and below by a floral one. Added
separately to this moulded part of the
bowl, the rim and the base were
wheel-made. According to the stamp,
the bowl was made by the potter Reg-
inus in the Rheinzabern manufacture.

Terra sigillata is the most important
type of Roman pottery. It can be
dated quite precisely and therefore
supplies important clues for archae-

ologists. As this pottery was bought mainly by the Roman army, the manufactures were moved to shorten the transport from Italy (Arezzo, Puteoli) to the south of France (La Gaufesenque), central France (Lezoux) and eventually also to Germany (Rheinzabern). The pottery was traded beyond the Roman Empire as far as non-Roman Germany. This terra sigillata bowl found near Leihgestern (near Giessen) presumably also got there through trade.

MK

ends in a rosette and supports a drop-shaped emerald. A pyramidal hood made of sheet gold was slipped over the wire. The hood and a strip of sheet gold shaped into a double volute at its peak are attached to the loop with a strip of sheet gold decorated with a granulated bead.

The tombs found in Pantikapaion on the Kerch' peninsula (Ukraine) are remarkable for their abundant jewellery. The combination of precious metal, pearls and precious stones was especially popular in the Roman Empire.

MK

Earrings with Emeralds
100–200 AD;
found in Pantikapaion
gold, pearls, emeralds,
H 4.6 cm – Inv. no.V 112
gift of Curt Luckow 1975

The earrings are in two parts, one solidly mounted and one movable. Attached to a thin gold wire equipped with a hook and a loop is a bowl-like concave gold disk with a fluted edge. Fastened inside it by a pin ending in a rosette, is a pearl surrounded by a twisted rope of gold wire. Another wire, attached to the lower loop, forms a freely dangling pendant. It also

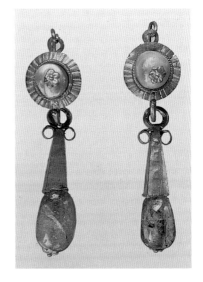

Imperium Romanum

Late Roman Empire
200–330 AD

Jupiter

200–300 AD
bronze, cast, H 10 cm – Inv. no. Br 38
purchased about 1777

Shown in heroic nudity, the god wears a chlamys draped across his left shoulder and falling to the backs of his knees. He leans on the (missing) sceptre in his raised right hand while his lowered left holds a bundle of lightning bolts. The bearded face of the god is framed with thick protruberant curls. This bronze, based on a representation of Jupiter according to the Classical canon, was probably from a domestic shrine or a votive offering at a public sanctuary. For stylistic reasons, the rather summarily executed statue dates from as late as the 3rd century AD.   *MK*

Dionysos-Bacchus and the Seasons

about 250 AD; sarcophagus (front)
marble relief, B 211 cm – Inv. no. Sk 46
purchased 1777

For the Romans the four seasons always symbolised the fertility of nature in terms of growth and decay. In the sepulchral context their depiction means that the dead are to be presented with nature's gifts. On the front of this tub-shaped sarcophagus, the four seasons flank the youthful god Bacchus, the central figure, who rides towards the right on his panther. Scantily dressed, carrying his thyrsus (staff) in his left hand, the god pours wine from a beaker into a rhyton (drinking horn)

held out by Pan. The genies of the seasons, shown as winged youths, are nude except for a loosely draped mantle, held by a fibula on one shoulder, down to behind their knees. They are characterised by their customary attributes (far right: spring with a cornucopia, hares and a wreath of rosettes; inner right: summer with a sheaf of wheat, sickle [restored] and wreath of wheat ears; inner left: autumn with a basket with garlands of figs and a wreath of olive branches; outer left: winter with two ducks, cornucopia and wreath of reeds).

The sarcophagus was produced by an urban Roman workshop. A typical feature of the mid-3rd century AD is the densely crowding (horror vacui) of the relief with the Pan figures, satyrs, cupids, etc. of Bacchus's entourage between the main figures. The soft rounded forms and the deeply drilled curls also identify it as a masterly work of this period.   *MK*

Maximianus Herculius (O) – Farnese Hercules (R)

gold coin (quinar)
286–305 AD
(reigning Roman emperor)
gold, weight 3.18 g – Inv. no. Mü 683
purchased 1998

This gold coin minted in Rome shows the bust of Emperor Maximianus Herculius facing right on the obverse. His short haircut is crowned with a diadem of precious stones with long ribbons falling down the nape of his neck. The emperor is wearing armour. Represented on the reverse is the famous statue of Hercules in repose (the so-called Farnese Hercules), especially popular in Rome. Copies based

on this statue by the Greek sculptor Lysippos, who flourished in the 4th century BC, were set up in Rome in front of the baths founded by Caracalla.

In the Roman Empire, coins were a favourite means of propaganda for the rulers to depict government programs, personal virtues or political triumphs such as victories. The inscription, VIRTVS AVGG ("virtue of the emperors") should also be interpreted in this sense. Maximianus, as his cognomen indicates, had chosen the demigod Hercules as his personal guardian deity. His portrayal is meant to symbolise the close relationship between the emperor and the hero.   *MK*

Iulia Domna as Victoria

about 200 AD;
wife of the Roman Emperor
Septimius Severus
(reign 193–211 AD)
sardonyx cameo
H 16.3 cm – Inv. no. Ge 236
purchased from the Capello collection,
Venice 1700–1710

The Empress Iulia Domna shown on
the cameo is unmistakably characterised by her attributes as Victoria, the
goddess of victory. Seated on a pile of
weapons, in which a shield, helmet
with plume, and breastplate can be
identified, she uses a round shield as
a footstool. Other typical attributes
of Victoria are the victor's wreath in
her right hand, the palm of victory in
her left arm and her wings. Over her
high-belted chiton, the Empress-
goddess wears a mantle.

When Roman emperors had
themselves portrayed as gods, it was
basically to serve propaganda. Imperial gifts to members of the Roman
upper class at festive occasions such as
the New Year, gems and cameos of
this kind were to illustrate the rulers'
confidence in their divine protection
and support. Sometimes the images
refer to political events of the day.
Thus this cameo would have been
made soon after the accession of Emperor Septimus Severus, when he,
having had to compete with four
other heirs to the throne, still had to
legitimise his rule.   *MK*

The Survival
of the Classics
Replicas, Models, Casts

Youth of Pesaro ("Idolino")

30 BC, Florence Mus. Arch.
bronze, cast, patinated,
H 150.5 cm – Inv. no. N 8
cast replica about 1730 (?)
purchased in Genoa 1756

The Kassel statue of the "Idolino"
(little idol) is a cast bought in Italy in
1756 of a bronze statue found in 1530
in Pesaro and now preserved in Florence. The nude boy looks pensively,
his head slightly bent, at a (missing)
sacrificial dish (phiale) that he holds in
his outstretched right hand. His left
arm hangs down loosely. As it depicts
a sacrifice, the statue probably belongs
in a ritual context.

In Hellenistic Roman fashion
(Roman Classicism), the original had
adopted exemplary formal elements
from older Greek prototypes. While
the head, with its firmly set features
and schematic curls, is influenced by

statues of athletes by the sculptor Polyclitus of about 450 BC, archaeologists date the body, with its fluid swaying rhythm, by stylistic comparisons to the 4th century BC. In the Kassel replica, the head and the body are no longer that incongruous because the prototype's components were reworked and adjusted by the bronze founder during the casting process. *MK*

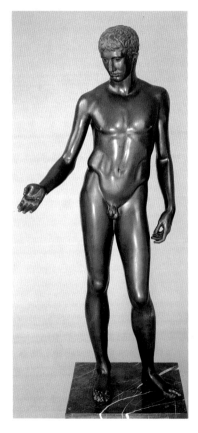

Pyramid of Cestius
model by Antonio Chichi 1777–82
wood, cork, stucco, painted,
H 71 cm – Inv. no. N 116
purchased in Rome 1777–82

The 36.4-metre-high pyramid shaped tomb in Rome has a square base (the sides are 29.5 m long). The core structure of cast stone (opus caementicium) has travertine panels cladding the base and marble ones above. A 10-metre-long hall led from the west to the barrel-vaulted tomb chamber, 6 x 4 m in size. Both were clad in brick, the chamber covered with what are now completely faded paintings in the so-called Third Style. Only the bases of the two statues of the dead beside the entrance have been preserved. Inscriptions on plaques on the east and west sides of the pyramid name Gaius Cestius Epulo as the owner of the tomb. Registered as a full citizen of Rome in the Publilia electoral district, he held public office as a praetor, tribune, and septemvir epulonum (member of a priesthood to perform ritual feasts). In his will Cestius disposed that his tomb be completed in less than 330 days. The tomb is dated to 18–12 BC because Marcus Agrippa, a counsellor and son-in-law of Augustus, who died that year, is still listed as an heir.

The tomb ranks among the series of Egyptian-style buildings that became very popular in Rome after the conquest of Egypt in 30 BC. Originally erected in the Roman cemetery on Via Ostiensis, it became part of the Aurelian wall in 271 AD and thus escaped destruction. In 1663 the pyramid was exposed and restored. At that time two of the four columns originally on the corners were set up

along the western side. They have been omitted, however, in the cork model. *MK*

Athena Lemnia
plaster cast, metal plated; Dresden 1914–1966/Kassel 1993
Roman copy about 100 AD of a Greek original about 450 BC
attrib. to Phidias
plaster replica, metal-plated,
H of the figure 200 cm – Inv. no. N 142

The statue known as Athena Lemnia probably transmits a sculpture by Phidias in the mature Classical style of about 450 BC that was set up on the Acropolis. The Roman marble copy dated about 100 AD shows the contained but animated impression, with the limited movement, closed silhouette and idealised features, of the Classical Greek bronze.

The youthfully slim goddess wears a peplos. Over it she has belted the aegis around her waist with a snake. The heavy folds of the drapery fall in parallel lines, bunching under her right armpit, interrupted only by her slightly bent left knee. The face of the Gorgon on the aegis is strictly symmetrical. Snakes curl along the hem of the aegis. The goddess's middle-parted, short, curly hair protrudes in the form of a wreath under her hairband, framing her face. Athena is rarely shown without her helmet.

The replica has restored the lance in Athena's raised left hand and the helmet in her right, her arm bent outward to the side, which the goddess is looking at. The cast, made from a plaster reconstruction in Dresden, was bronze-plated and the aegis silver-plated. This brilliant colourful effect would not have lasted long after the original was set up on the Acropolis in Athens. Bronze statues, especially outdoors, patinate after a while to a dark greenish black hue. *MK*

reworked on the replica in order to obtain the taut surface typical of bronzes. The whole statue was then bronze-plated with high-quality metal. The eyes are framed with sheet copper eyelashes, their pupils inlaid with blue glass paste. Lips and nipples were modelled in bronze; the bow was plated with silver steel. Added to the replica is a migratory locust, based on ancient and zoological representations and triply enlarged, which the god seems to grip lightly in his right hand. The Kassel Apollo possibly shows the statue of Apollo Parnopios (protector against locusts) that Phidias made for the Athens Acropolis. The god had this cognomen because he apparently freed the country's population from a plague of locusts.   *MK*

The Kassel Apollo

Plaster cast, metal plated; Kassel 1991
Roman copy about 100 AD of a
Greek original about 450 BC
attrib. to Phidias
plaster, metal-plated,
H of the figure 200 cm – Inv. no. N 138

When we look at white marble statues it is hard to imagine the polychromy of the ancient originals or the effect that golden statues made of bronze would have had. In order to recreate this impression, a bronze-plated replica was made of the best-preserved statue in Kassel, the Apollo by Phidias.

First the typical changes added by ancient marble sculptors when they copied a hollow-cast bronze original were removed from the plaster cast of the statue, i.e. the marble bars or supports added in particularly fragile areas. Individual parts such as the head, joints, hands and feet were also

The Farnese Hercules

plaster cast 1990; Roman copy
about 220 AD in Naples
signed GLYKON ATHENAIOS
EPOIESEN; from a Greek original
about 320 BC
attrib. to Lysippos
H of the figure 301 cm – Inv. no. A 388
purchased 1992

Representations of Hercules were popular in antiquity because the life of the hero offered a wide variety of aspects for illustration – besides virtuous qualities and heroic deeds, numerous vices of the hero were reported.

One of the most frequently copied works of art showing Hercules is the so-called Farnese type. The original, by the Greek sculptor Lysippos of about 320 BC, was copied in the early 3rd century AD by Glykon the Athenian, presumably for the baths of Caracalla in Rome.

Hercules, resting from his exploits, has put down his club, with a lion's skin draped over it, on a rock and leans on it with his left arm. The hero's right hand is behind his back, holding the apples that he has taken from the Hesperides in the latest of his heroic labours. While the fruits symbolise happiness and immortality, the statue itself can be interpreted very differently: both as an image of a powerful hero and a symbol of repose after accomplishing heroic deeds.

The heavy muscular body and details such as the springy hair and the theatrical downward gaze were very popular in the art of the Hellenistic period.

Found in 1546 and named after the Palazzo Farnese where it was exhibited, the statue was considered the prototype of a perfectly proportioned colossus and was therefore frequently copied, all the way up to the 19th century. *MK*

The Old Masters
Art Gallery

History of the Old Masters Art Gallery

Bernhard Schnackenburg

Among the great European picture galleries, there are two distinct historic types: the 17th- and 18th-century collections established by princes, and the 19th- and 20th-century collections built up by museum professionals. While Berlin and London are major examples of the latter, Kassel has preserved a prince's picture collection of the Baroque era in relatively intact form. Unlike those in most other former residencies, it has retained, regardless of earlier or later acquisitions, the stamp of one personality: Landgrave Wilhelm VIII of Hesse-Kassel (1682–1760). His passion for collecting, distinguished by his outstanding connoisseurship and highly developed sense for quality, though also affected by contemporary taste, his personal connections and resources, has left a lasting mark on the Kassel art gallery. Its high rank is not based on the collection's being an evenly distributed representation of all schools and epochs, but on its magnificent concentrations and special points of focus, especially in Flemish and Dutch Baroque painting.

Commissions for paintings by the Kassel landgraves have been documented since the early 16th century. The first is a small triptych by Lucas Cranach the Elder (see p. 75), which Landgrave Wilhelm II (reign 1487–1509) or his widow commissioned around 1508–09, the first out-of-town commission for the court painter in Wittenberg. Probably given away during the Reformation, it did not return to Kassel until 1905, as a gift of the industrialist Dr. Ludwig Mond, a native of Kassel. Nothing survived in the gallery from the following century, until Landgrave Moritz the Learned (reign 1592–1627) again left behind traces in the collection. Probably dating back to his rule is an important group of Nuremberg portraits including works by Wolgemut, Dürer (see p. 72) and Beham. In 1603 his second wife Juliane of Nassau brought a group of family portraits with her to Kassel from Dillenburg. Outstanding among these is the portrait by Anthonis Mor (see p. 109) of her great-uncle William of Orange, the founder of the Protestant Dutch Republic. This is followed by another long epoch for which no acquisitions are documented, the period of the Thirty Years' War and its serious consequences particularly for Hesse.

Finally, under the politically and culturally distinguished Landgrave Karl (reign 1677–1730) there was a fresh impetus that also had an effect on painting. When the prince died in 1730 an inventory was made of his paintings in the "high-princely cabinet" and the "new cabinet" of the palace of his residence. His collection in the Kunsthaus (art building) was considerably larger. Landgrave Karl had established this museum, which was inaugurated in 1709, in the Ottoneum, originally built as a theatre in 1604–05. It housed the collections of natural science, the picture cabinet and the collection of court portraits and other paintings that, in part, served only illustrative purposes. Much had been added to the core collection since the late 17th century. Yet it was not in any sense a systematically developed collection of paintings. Worthy of note, besides commissioned works (van Nikkelen, see p. 100; J.M. Roos, see p. 97), is a group of Flemish and Dutch artists (Van Balen, see p. 125) as well as contemporary Venetian painters (Damini, see p. 87) the prince had learned to appreciate during his trip to Italy in 1699–1700.

The actual founder of the gallery, Wilhelm VIII, was born in 1682 as the second son of Landgrave Karl. Because of political and religious as well as family ties to the house of Orange-Nassau, he spent several decades starting in 1703 in the army in the Netherlands, where he distinguished himself in battle in the War of the Spanish Succession. In those years he developed into a knowledgeable admirer of the culture of the Netherlands, which was to influence his taste for the rest of his life. His income as governor of the frontier fortresses of Breda and Maastricht from 1713 and 1723 on, respectively, permitted him to pursue his passion for collecting paintings. In 1716 there is already mention of a sizeable picture cabinet. At first "Prins Willem" seems to have been especially interested in contemporary painters, whose studios he visited and who put him in touch with collectors and art dealers. His aim to set up a universal collection of paintings first became evident in 1722, when he bid at the Rotterdam Jacques Meijers auction not only for paintings by Van Poelenburch and Wouwerman, but also by Italian and French masters (Bourdon, see p. 93).

After the death of Landgrave Karl, Wilhelm, who had already resided mainly in Kassel the preceding years, took over governmental affairs as the governor for his older brother, Landgrave Friedrich I, who had become the King of Sweden through marriage and was residing in Stockholm. Only after the latter's death in 1751 did Wilhelm VIII become the reigning landgrave. As the regent of Kassel he stepped up his collecting activities, mainly by making use of his Dutch contacts. Many paintings were exhibited in his private palace in Frankfurter Strasse (destroyed in 1943), where the banqueting hall was decorated with four large paintings by Jacob Jordaens, including the *Family Portrait* and *The Satyr Visiting the Peasant* (see pp. 135 and 136).

These paintings had possibly already been bought in the Netherlands. As with most acquisitions, there is no documentation. The first reference is often in the inventory of Wilhelm VIII's paintings. Made in 1749 and carried forth to the end of his reign for new acquisitions, it is still used as the major authority today. However, a number of important accessions can be traced in Dutch auction catalogues of this period. The altarpiece and the *Flight into Egypt* by Rubens (see pp. 129 and 140) came from Amsterdam auctions of 1734 and 1735. Correspondence dating from 1738 with the Amsterdam art dealer Antonie Rutgers has been preserved. He sold the Krul portrait by Rembrandt to Kassel and the church interior by Saenredam (see p. 116), as a companion-piece to an existing one by the Flemish painter Neefs. Pairs of pictures were very much in demand in the Baroque era and were even assembled artificially. They were indispensable for the symmetrical hangings fashionable at the time.

Wilhelm VIII's gallery, 1751–1877 (photograph of 1934 renovations; destroyed 1943)

The most intensive phase of collection building began in 1748. It was during this period that the Kassel gallery attained European rank. The most important market continued to be Holland, but Wilhelm VIII spread his sphere of activities to Paris, Brussels, Antwerp, Venice and German cities such as Frankfurt and Hamburg, where his diplomats and art agents were on the lookout for pictures. His most important advisors and confidants were the Frankfurt collector Baron von Häckel, the collector Govert van Slingeland, and the art dealer Gerard Hoet in The Hague, and in Kassel the Gallery Inspector von Freese and Lieutenant General August Moritz von Donop. At the beginning of the year Häckel mediated the acquisition of two small-sized group portraits by Gonzales Coques (see p. 110). The attribution and the deciphering of the unfamiliar signature led to a lively correspondence that demonstrates Wilhelm's profound interests. In 1749 a shipment of six first-class paintings arrived from Gerard Hoet, including the full-figure *Portrait of a Spaniard* and the *Portrait of Sebastian Leerse with his Wife and Son* by Anthony van Dyck (see pp. 130 and 133). The energetic, internationally busy Hoet also procured the highlight of the Rubens collection, the *The Victor's Triumph* (see p. 128) through clever negotiations with the original patron, the militia company of St George in Antwerp. Just to make sure, Wilhelm VIII had Hoet's offers examined, insofar as he did not have them sent to himself for review, by the highly esteemed expert Slingeland, who was also a buyer himself. In the same year he increased the already substantial Wouwerman holdings in Kassel by two works, including the *The Piebald at the Forge* (see p. 120). This Dutch painter was extremely highly regarded in the 18th century, and the Kassel gallery still has twenty of his paintings today! The important family portrait by Marten van Heemskerck (see p. 107) was purchased in Paris. It was ascribed to Hans Holbein the Younger at the time.

As the rooms available for the rapidly growing collection became too small, Wilhelm VIII had the Munich court architect François de Cuvilliés the Elder, who also designed the summer residence, Wilhelmsthal Palace, plan annexes for his palace in town. New residential and banqueting rooms in Frankfurter Strasse and Bellevue Strasse (or *An der Schönen Aussicht*, meaning *At the Beautiful View*) were to be linked by means of three gallery wings. This grandiose planning, however, could only be realised in part. From 1749 to 1751 a gallery wing was built in Fünffensterstrasse, which was ruined in 1943. While construction was in progress, Marquis d'Argenson was visiting in Kassel. One of the major Parisian connoisseurs and collectors, he procured several pictures for the prince, including Rottenhammer's *Ecce Homo* (see p. 126).

Offers from Paris continued to be particularly interesting in the years to follow. In early 1750 a capital Teniers was bought there from Marshal Isenghien "for a big pile of money": the large *Peasant Dance by a Tavern* (see p. 134). Hoet procured a picture by the no less esteemed peasant painter Adriaen van Ostade, with the popular title *Merry Country Folk* (see p. 122). In a letter written in May, the prince gave the number of his paintings as 527, excluding the portraits, which were not counted as holdings of the gallery. But only 200 to 300 were really good, he added self-critically. As early as August, this number was to be increased substantially. After months of negotiations, conducted in secret for fear of competition, with the help of Slingeland and Hoet, he succeeded in purchasing the complete collection of paintings of the deceased Delft collector Valerius Röver; 64 paintings, most of them first class, came into Kassel's possession. The price of 40,000 guild-ers plus 3% commission for Hoet was suitable, as the Röver art cabinet was considered the greatest private collection in Holland. Among the eight works by Rembrandt were the *Old Man with a Gold Chain*, the *Portrait of a Man Sharpening a Quill* and *Saskia in Profile* (see pp. 146, 147 and 148), the *Self-Portrait with Helmet* and the *Portrait of Nicolaes Bruyningh*. This group of works, whose quality and artistic variety Wilhelm never tired of extolling, made the Kassel collection of Rembrandts the biggest of its day. Other remarkable Dutch paintings in this sale are by Jan Steen (*Twelfth Night*, see p. 121), Abraham Mignon and Frans van Mieris the Younger (see p. 121); of note among Italian school are major works by Francesco Bassano (see p. 81), Palma il Giovane (see p. 81) and Giuseppe Cesari (see p. 82).

Wilhelm VIII now intended to take a break in collecting, but the year 1751 was once again filled with important acquisitions. Gerard Hoet obtained the *Cock-Fight* and the *White Peacock* by Melchior de Hondecoeter (see p. 146), the Respaigne portrait by Rubens and the two paintings of Venus, in artificial light and daylight, by Godfried Schalcken (see p. 113). Wilhelm's friend in Frankfurt, Baron Häckel, with whom he carried on an intensive exchange of ideas, obtained a masterpiece of Venetian Baroque painting, Bellucci's *The Sick Prince* (see p. 85) for him from the estate of Privy Counsellor Pfeiff of the Electorate of Mainz.

When the new gallery room was set up, some paintings from his father's art museum (Kunsthaus) were included. To decorate the room, the landgrave commissioned four overdoor pieces with the allegories of the seasons from

Jacob de Wit in Amsterdam (see p. 95), which were delivered in 1751 and 1752. The two allegories of art by the Venetian Giuseppe Nogari were acquired at the same time directly from the artist (see p. 96). Wilhelm VIII's interest in contemporary art is demonstrated most clearly in 1752 when he discovered Johann Heinrich Tischbein, who had begun his career in Mainz after training abroad. Wilhelm VIII appointed this painter, who had unexpected abilities for a German and, morever, came from the vicinity of Kassel, as his court painter. He commissioned the two mythological paintings, *The Mocking of Anacreon* (see p. 95) and *Hercules and Omphale* expressly for the new art gallery.

In 1752 the Rembrandt collection was enlarged for the last time. Gerhard Morell, a Danish art dealer working in Hamburg, furnished the *Full-Length Portrait of a Standing Gentleman*, Hoet the *Winter Landscape*, and an unknown seller *Jacob Blessing the Sons of Joseph* (see p. 145). The latter did not become the most famous masterpiece of the Kassel gallery until the 19th century. Wilhelm VIII, who had many contacts in The Hague, bought the *Holy Family with a Curtain* (see p. 157) directly from the large collection of Willem Lormier, as well as Netscher's *Masquerade Joke* (see p. 118) and Breenbergh's *Landscape with Ruins and Saints Peter and John* (see p. 142). The Jordaens collection also grew to outstanding proportions and rank through the purchase of *Twelfth Night* (see p. 137) from the Berlin Counsellor of Commerce Triebel, and the *Childhood of Jupiter* (see p. 138) from the painter Anton Kappers in Münster. Triebel was also the source of the second genre paint-

ing in Kassel by Frans Hals, the *Singing Boys*. His famous *Peeckelhaeringh* (see p. 144) had already been in the collection since 1749.

From 1753 on, news about new acquisitions becomes scarce, but it does concern a number of masterpieces. The huge Janssens (see p. 130) came to Kassel from the Frankfurt painter Johann Benjamin Ehrenreich, and, at about the same time, one of the most beautiful works of the Late Gothic period in Amsterdam, *Noli me tangere* by Jacob Cornelisz. van Oostsanen (see p. 106). This name had actually been forgotten and was replaced by an attribution to Albrecht Dürer. The acquisition of 10 decorative paintings, most of them large, by Adriaen van der Werff directly from the painter's heirs must have been a special source of satisfaction for the landgrave. The middle one of the three ceiling paintings, *Flora with Putti Scattering Flowers* gave today's new central room on the first storey its name. Subsequent entries in the inventory include a remarkable number of Italian paintings of the late Baroque period, such as the two by Piazzetta (see p. 87), *Caritas* by Franceschini (see p. 88), *Bathsheba* by Pietro Liberi and other large pictures by Antonio Bellucci and Antonio Molinari. On 15 June 1753 Wilhelm VIII wrote to Baron Häckel: "I am gradually obtaining the necessary material for a gallery of Italian works ... If only there were also a building for it!" He was probably thinking of one of the unrealised gallery wings behind his palace in town.

Three paintings figure as the important conclusion of Wilhelm VIII's collecting activities: Giampietrino's *Leda* (see p. 77) and Titian's *Portrait of a Commander-in-Chief* (see p. 79) were bought in Paris in 1756. The former, transformed into a *Caritas* by over-painting and ascribed to Leonardo, was considered the most important painting in Kassel until it was lost in 1806; its repurchase succeeded in 1962. The extraordinary Titian portrait became the undisputed highlight of the Italian collection. At the same time *The Man in a Slouch Hat* by Frans Hals (see p. 144), one of the most well known works by the famous Haarlem portraitist, was purchased from an unknown "M. Tarno." Long before this painter was rediscovered in the 19th century, he was valued and collected by Wilhelm VIII. The outbreak of the Seven Years' War in 1756 prevented further acquisitions. Hesse-Kassel was allied with Prussia, and when the French occupied the landgraviate in the following year, the seventy-five-year-old landgrave escaped; he died in Rinteln on the River Weser in 1760.

Landgrave Friedrich II (reign 1760–1785) developed similar interests in his youth under the guidance of his father. The latter praised the growing expertise of the hereditary prince and his purchase of a Rembrandt in a letter to Baron Häckel in 1748. Several paintings, some of them highlights of the gallery, which go back to Friedrich may have been bought in this early period. These include the *Large River Landscape with a Windmill* by Rembrandt, two small portraits of gentlemen by Frans Hals, a couple making music by Gerard ter Borch (see p. 119), *Appelles and the Cobbler* by Frans Francken the Younger (see p. 127), the landscape by Jacques d'Arthois (see p. 135) and the large Murillo, *Joseph and Potiphar's Wife* (see p. 91). But when the prince's secret conversion to Catholicism became known in 1754 and led to a split with his father, Friedrich stopped following his example. Instead, he became an important collector of antiquities. For his new acquisitions and the collections of his grandfather in the art museum he set up the Museum Fridericianum, which was opened in 1779.

This large-scale museum was planned from the start not for the princely household but for the public. Friedrich II, a prince of the Age of Enlightenment, even included the famous gallery of paintings in his cultural reforms. In 1775 it was opened to a select public, often visitors who had travelled from afar. Their guide was the recently appointed Gallery Inspector

Gallery "An der Schönen Aussicht," 1877–1939 (Neue Galerie since 1976)

Johann Heinrich Tischbein the Younger, a nephew of the court painter. When the landgrave founded an academy of painting and sculpture in 1777, the collection of paintings was included in the programme of studies and many pictures wandered over into the rooms of the academy. The first printed catalogue of the gallery, by Professor Simon Causid of Marburg University, was published in 1783.

In 1803 Landgrave Wilhelm IX (reign 1785–1821, from 1803 as Prince Elector Wilhelm I), who did not stand out as a collector of paintings, acquired Ribera's *Mater Dolorosa* (see p. 90) from the Bavarian prince elector in exchange for a picture by Paulus Potter. The major turning point during his reign was Napoleonic foreign rule, during which time the picture gallery suffered serious losses. Evacuated in headlong haste to the hunting lodge of Sababurg in 1806 to hide them from the advancing French, 48 major works were captured as spoils of war. Most of them became the property of Empress Joséphine, whose heirs sold them to the Tzar in 1814. Paintings by Claude Lorrain, Andrea del Sarto, Rembrandt, Potter, Teniers and others that had constituted the main claim to fame of the Kassel gallery, thus came to be part of the collection of the Hermitage in St Petersburg; others went to London. In 1807 Vivant Denon, the director of the Musée Napoléon, seized the rest of the masterpieces among the gallery's holdings, 299 paintings that were shown in the Louvre in 1808. Napoleon's younger brother Jérôme, who resided in Kassel as the King of Westphalia, was careless with the remaining works; many items were stolen and misappropriated. The empty gallery room was given other uses and subdivided into smaller rooms. When Jérôme had to escape in 1813 he took 165 paintings with him, only a few of which returned. After the end of the French Empire, while the Hessian delegation headed by Jakob Grimm was able to recoup 418 paintings from Paris and the French provinces, a thorough stock-taking by the new Gallery Inspector Ernst Friedrich Ferdinand Robert registered a loss of 382 pictures. After the annexation of the former Prince Bishopric of Fulda, a group of paintings came from there to Kassel in 1816. Outstanding among these is the *Great Flood* by Johann Heinrich Schönfeld (see p. 99).

The return of Kassel's paintings on 1 November 1815 was cause for a public celebration but it did not result in a fresh start for the gallery. The prince elector left the subdivisions standing in the gallery, and had the pictures housed somehow in those low and small rooms. Under him and his successors the building became increasingly derelict, access was made difficult, important works were withdrawn to decorate the palaces. Cultural tradition had reverted to princely private property. Prince Elector Wilhelm II (reign 1821–1831) did, however, devote himself to collecting, particularly contemporary painting, for a few years. Most of his acquisitions of earlier works came from the Leipzig Campe auction of 1827, such as the All Saints altarpiece by Oostsanen, landscapes by Aert van der Neer and Allaert van Everdingen and the *Portrait of Philip de Flines* by Gerard de Lairesse (see p. 112). Under the last Prince Elector Friedrich Wilhelm (reign 1831–1866) the gallery fell into a long sleep. Martin Schaffner's extraordinary painted table-top (see p. 74), escaping public notice, ended up in the Museum Fridericianum after 1834 by inheritance from a collateral branch of the reigning family.

After the end of the Electorate of Hesse-Kassel in 1866, the new Prussian government brought about a revival. As the paintings had already suffered damages in the badly kept facilities, a new building paid for with the fortune of the former ruler was planned in the neighbourhood. 1877 saw the move to the new gallery building "An der Schönen Aussicht." In the same year the gallery was given its first scholarly director, Oscar Eisenmann. In spite of limited resources from Berlin, he took advantage of the economic prosperity of the times and the importance of Kassel as the imperial summer residence for some important new acquisitions. He advised the Kassel industrialist and art lover Edward Habich on his purchases, took over Habich's collection as a loan, and was finally able to obtain 23 paintings when it was dissolved in 1892, four of them as gifts from Habich and nine from Emperor Wilhelm II. These accessions include Baldung's *Hercules and Antaeus* (see p. 72), ter Brugghen's *Flute Players* (see p. 155), de Grebber's *Belshazzar's Feast* (see p. 145) and a large marine landscape by de Vlieger (see p. 115). Among the other Dutch paintings, a *Winter Landscape* by Esaias van de Velde (see p. 158) and a still-life with game by Frans Snyders (see p. 140) are remarkable. The most important new Italian acquisitions were two wings of an altarpiece by Romanino (see p. 76) in 1896. The collection of early German painting, comprising only a few individual works so far, was expanded by Eisenmann into a small separate department with Schaffner's

painted table as its central focus. The Bubenhoven epitaph by the Master of Messkirch was bought in 1887, and Altdorfer's expressive *Crucifixion* (see p. 73) in 1905.

Eisenmann's successor Georg Gronau renovated the gallery's rooms in 1911 and thinned out the crowded walls, where pictures had been hanging in several rows one above the other. With his limited resources for new acquisitions, he concentrated on the German 18th and the Dutch 17th centuries, among which the *Singing Audition* by Jacob Ochtervelt (see p. 119) was particularly fortuitous. When Gronau retired in 1924, the Prussian government did not fill the vacancy but merged the gallery and the Hessisches Landesmuseum (Museum of the Land of Hesse) to form the Staatliche Kunstsammlungen (State Art Collections; since 1992: State Museums) Kassel.

Possibilities for reorganisation presented themselves for the director of the state art collections under a broader roof. When the gallery's rooms were renovated once more in 1934 and hung in a modern fashion according to a scale still applied today by emphasising major individual works of art, the 19th-century building became too small for the entire collection. Many paintings, especially the large-sized Italian ones, moved over into the newly founded neighbouring Landgrafenmuseum (Landgrave's Museum), whose festive focus was Wilhelm VIII's gallery hall, now freed of its subdivisions from Jérôme's days. This museum lasted only until 1939. In 1943 the historic buildings were destroyed by bombs.

In World War II the gallery suffered many losses through fire, theft and the

Hessisches Landesmuseum (Museum of the Land of Hesse), selected exhibition on the 1st floor, 1945–1973

plundering of evacuation sites, but fortunately not among the masterpieces. The gallery building "An der Schönen Aussicht" (Neue Galerie since 1976) was heavily damaged in 1943, when 800 frames also went up in flames. In 1945 the paintings had to be stored in the only intact museum building left in Kassel, the Hessisches Landesmuseum. That very year saw the first of a series of small selected exhibitions, followed in 1949 by a provisional permanent display on the main storey, which ended up lasting almost a quarter of a century. The main event in these years was the return in 1956 of 63 masterpieces from Vienna, which had been evacuated there in 1942 and could only be released by the Soviet Union after the signing of the Austrian constitution (1955). After years of discussion on where to rebuild the gallery, whether "An der Schönen Aussicht,"

Museum Fridericianum, or Schloss Wilhelmshöhe, the provincial government of Hesse decided in 1960 in favour of the gutted palace halfway up Habichtswald, despite misgivings due to its considerable distance from the city centre. Construction began in 1963 and dragged on. Meanwhile, a number of important permanent loans from the Federal Republic of Germany could be accessed in 1966 and 1969, including works by Jacopo Tintoretto (*Lot and his Daughters*, see p. 80) and Giulio Carpioni (*The Blind Seer Tiresias*, see p. 85). The Italian department, which was to be given more weight in the future, was also strengthened by purchases such as the animal still-life by Giacomo Ceruti (see p. 86). The Flemish school received a new emphasis on the 16th century with a major early work by Frans Floris *The Judgement of Paris* (see p. 108);

Schloss Wilhelmshöhe Museum, site of the gallery since 1974

a notable new accession among the Dutch 17th-century works was the *Italian Seaport* by Jan Weenix (see p. 114). Schloss Wilhelmshöhe Museum was opened at last in 1974, with the collection of Greek and Roman antiquities on the ground storey and three storeys of galleries above. Regardless of heavy criticism of the deliberately avant-garde interior design by Paul-Friedrich Posenenske, which countered the symmetries and statics of the 18th-century architecture, the new museum soon began to appeal to the public. The unique ensemble of a palace, mountain-park, and art centre became the showpiece of Kassel and a very popular tourist attraction.

Several years' experience indicated that it would be a good idea to thin out the hanging some more, and to set up a study gallery instead with pictures hung closely together in rows one above the other. The collection policy's main objective from the 80s on was to fill obvious gaps in the core collection, i.e. the Rembrandt school. The purchase of a portrait of a gentleman by Jacob Adriansz. Backer in 1984 was followed in 1987 with that of *the Portrait of Margaretha Tulp as a Bride* by Govaert Flinck (see p. 150), in 1989 with the scene closely related to Rembrandt, *Christ and the Woman Taken in Adultery* by Gerbrand van den Eeckhout (see p. 151), and in 1993–94 with a cycle of four *Allegories of the Elements and the Ages of Man* by the young Jan Lievens (see p. 156). In addition, the piece by piece acquisition since the 70s of the cycle of *The Seasons* by Ignaz Stern (see p. 99) was completed. These pictures as well as the very early *Mountain Valley* by Pieter Stevens (see p. 124) were generous gifts from the company B. Braun of Melsungen.

The successful operation of the museum was not able to obscure the fact that considerable interior architectural and structural problems were leading to increasingly impaired aesthetics and conservation. Thus the gallery had to be closed in 1994. For six long years it had to make do with selective temporary exhibitions, first in the Museum Fridericianum and later in the Neue Galerie and the Landesmuseum. Planning for the renovation began in 1993, in the course of which the commission went to the reputed Munich museum architect Stephan Braunfels. The basic idea of his consistently museum-oriented roof design presented in 1994 was to replace the former dome, which used to emphasise the centre of the broad palace ensemble, with a tall top-lit upper floor. This 'lantern storey' had to be realised in a considerably lower form. Nevertheless, it allows the five sky-lighted rooms to attain a height that is higher than any available in the rooms of the gallery to date.

With the re-opening of the Kassel art gallery in the summer of 2000 begins a new era of its centuries-old history. At last it can present its rich collections on its established site in appropriate rooms! About 500 paintings are exhibited, with 90 others in the study gallery, altogether about two thirds of the entire collection. The top-lit storey is devoted to the Flemish and Dutch masters. The itinerary leads through the five rooms along a central axis from Rubens through Van Dyck, with Jordaens in the centre, to Frans Hals and finally Rembrandt. The eight adjacent top-lit cabinets contain small paintings by these masters and works by their pupils and schools. In the two storeys below, the formerly irritating supporting pillars in the walls have made way for clearly structured rooms. The display of paintings from the Netherlands with its many small works continues in the low second storey, where a ring of 10 side-lit cabinets and four corner rooms encircles a large, artificially lit room that can be subdivided in various ways for special exhibitions. The adjoining Verbinderbau (connecting tract) houses the study gallery, as in the past. The first storey, the original bel-étage of the palace, displays paintings from Germany as well as Italy, France and Spain. Carefully taking daylight conditions into consideration, the four rooms on the side of the building facing town, which have plenty of light, were built to be deeper than the four on the park side with less light. In the centre is a room that is the full width of the palace, with views of both the city and the park. The festive Flora Room named after the three large ceiling paintings by Adriaen van der Werff showing Flora, the goddess of spring, with children scattering flowers, also contains works commissioned by the founder of the gallery, Landgrave Wilhelm VIII, as well as his portrait. In the connecting tract adjacent to the north, German painting of the 17th and early 18th centuries continues up to the Rococo period and early Neo-Classicism, where the emphasis is on Johann Heinrich Tischbein.

First Floor

Albrecht Dürer
1471 Nuremberg – 1528 Nuremberg

Portrait of Elsbeth Tucher 1499
limewood panel, 29.1 x 23.3 cm – GK 6

Portraits of burghers up to the early 16th century were customarily this small. One of the best known German Renaissance portraits, it long graced the twenty-mark bank notes of the Federal Republic of Germany. In 1499 the Tucher brothers Nikolaus and Hans had themselves and their wives painted in Nuremberg by Dürer. The pairs of portraits of the couples were not wall decoration but, hinged together originally, formed diptychs that could be opened and closed. While the pictures of Hans and Felicitas have been preserved (Schlossmusuem Weimar), Nikolaus Tucher's was lost. The initials NT on the clasp of Elsbeth's dress and the wedding ring she holds up refer to her husband. The inscription above reads: ELSPET NICLAS TVCHERN 26 ALT 1499 (26 years old). The letters MHIMNSK on the ribbon of her head-dress remain unexplained. Displayed next to Elsbeth Tucher's portrait is that of her mother-in-law, Ursula Tucher, painted by Dürer's teacher Michael Wolgemut in 1478. Comparison with this Late Gothic work shows up Dürer's firm sculptural modelling, the sitter's steady gaze towards her facing partner, and the rich, gold brocade background with a landscape view. *BS*

Hans Baldung, known as Grien
1484/85 Schwäbisch-Gmünd – 1545 Strasbourg

Hercules and Antaeus, 1531
lindenwood panel, 153.5 x 63.5 cm – GK 7

Two signatures appear on this painting: DIVO HERCVLI/1531/HBG at the top right and 1531/HG BALDVNG (VS)FAC at the lower left. Against a neutral dark background, it shows the mythical wrestling match between the Libyan giant Antaeus and the Greek hero and demi-god Hercules.

The Greek scholar Apollodorus (2nd half of the 2nd century BC) tells the story that Antaeus, the son of Gaea (the earth), challenged each foreigner to a match. Thanks to the strength he drew from the earth, he was invincible. Hercules, who knew his secret, lifted him up with all his might and was thus able to squeeze the giant to death in his arms. From the Christian and hu-

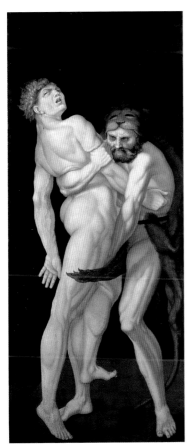

manistic point of view this act stood for the triumph of virtue over the brute force of nature.

With the precise depiction of the two male nudes in extremely violent action, and the protruding muscles, tendons and veins, Baldung puts his study of anatomy to the test. It had taken many years, e.g. his apprenticeship to Dürer in Nuremberg was 1503–06. Baldung was the leading master in the southwest of Germany until mid-century.   *JML*

Albrecht Altdorfer

about 1480 Regensburg (?) –
1538 Regensburg

Crucifixion with the Virgin
and Saint John, about 1512
limewood panel, 101.5 x 116 cm – GK 10a

This Crucifixion panel was an epitaph that once marked a family tomb in a Regensburg church or cloister. The coat of arms of the unidentified patrons, a hexagram, can be seen between the kneeling donors below. The numbers "88 X" below the trimmed INRI tablet on the cross (standing for Iesus Nazarenus Rex Iudaeorum, i.e. Jesus of Nazareth, King of the Jews), refer to the despairing Psalm 88, verse 10. The symmetry of the group is based on the layout of canon tables in medieval missals. The expressive figures reflect the influence of Mantegna and Dürer. The Virgin, addressing the viewer, gestures plaintively towards the Saviour, His body covered with blood, while St John turns away, inviting us to contemplation. Clouds cover the sun at the hour of Jesus's death. The splendid natural scenery of the foothills of the Alps with the colouring differen-

tiating between the fore-, middle- and background shows Altdorfer as a pioneer of landscape painting.　　　BS

Martin Schaffner
1478/79 Ulm (?) – after 1546 Ulm

Painted Table-Top for Erasmus Stedelin, 1533
limewood panel, 108.5 x 117.5 cm – GK 22

Martin Schaffner, the municipal painter of Ulm, used a tabletop as a surface on which to spread out an elaborate allegorical programme. The aim was not to decorate a piece of furniture, but to create a horizontal work of art. Painted table-tops of this kind were very popular at the time, especially in southern Germany. A small tablet held by a baby boy below the fortress on

the cliff-top names the patron, the Strassbourg goldsmith "asymus [=Erasmus] stedelin." It was probably the end of his apprenticeship that provided the occasion for Schaffner's painting. The "abc" that also appears on this tablet could then be understood as a humorous reference to the event. An open book a bit lower down also provides the year it was painted, "MDXXXIII". The connection between all the other images relates to the deep blue sky in the centre. Divine light radiates from the midst of a ring formed by the star-shaped symbol of the earth and the ancient symbols of the seven other planets of the cosmos. Opening out towards the edges of the table, the terrestrial part of the pictorial space is shown as a landscape, whose main figures correspond to the planets. The key figure is the ancient geographer Ptolemy, who is subordinate to the symbol of the earth and bears Schaffner's own facial features. His tablet states that the personifications of the seven liberal arts have gathered around him: grammar, rhetoric, arithmetic, logic, geometry, music and astronomy. Each has several additional attributes linking her to a colour, a metal, a Christian virtue, and one of the seven days of the week. A multitude of plants, animals, buildings and depictions of human labours fills the surrounding landscape with astonishing detail and variety.   *HJC*

Lucas Cranach the Elder
1472 Kronach – 1553 Weimar

Small Triptych with the Resurrection of Christ, about 1508/09
panel, central panel 38 x 25.8. cm, side panels 39 x 9.9 cm each – GK 11

This small triptych is still in its original 16th-century frame. This is the earliest known painting that was commissioned by the Kassel court. It was completed by one of the most famous German artists of his day, Lucas Cranach the Elder, court painter in Wittenberg. Presumably with reference to the

imminent (or lately occurred) death of Landgrave Wilhelm II, he painted the Biblical scene of the Resurrection of Christ as anticipating the resurrection of all mortals on the day of the Last Judgement. The central panel is flanked by images of two of the fourteen auxiliary saints, St Barbara (left) and St Catherine (right). The coats of arms of Hesse and Mecklenburg, the home of Landgravine Anna, decorate the outer sides of both wings. Cranach's mastery shows especially in the balanced composition and the harmonious combination of colours.   *HJC*

Girolamo da Romano, known as Romanino

1484/87 Brescia – after 1559 Brescia

Saint Peter, about 1513/15
poplar panel, 118 x 62 cm – GK 503

Saint Paul, about 1513/15
poplar panel, 117 x 63 cm – GK 503b

The Princes of the Apostles, Peter and Paul stand close up to the front of the picture space in a deep mountain landscape. They hold their canonical attributes in their hands: the keys (St Peter) and the sword (St Paul). A bluish-white sky in pale gradations forms the backdrop for the two monumentally conceived figures.

The two panels originally formed the wings of an altarpiece painted by Romanino around 1513/15 for a church in Brescia or the vicinity. In the

choice of the principal colours (red and olive yellow for Peter, bluish grey and purplish red for Paul) the young artist shows that he is strongly influenced by Venetian models such as Giovanni Bellini, Giorgione and Titian. Romanino, who worked mainly in his native city of Brescia, painted impressive altarpieces and frescoes in Padua, Cremona and Trent.   *JML*

Giampietrino
dates unknown; active about 1520–1540 in Milan

Leda with her Children, about 1530/35
alder wood panel, 128 x 105.5 cm – GK 966

Leda, the daughter of the Aetolian king, was married to Tyndareus, King of Sparta. However, this did not stop Zeus, the father of the gods, from an amorous adventure with the beautiful young woman, whom he approached in the form of a swan. The fruit of this union was two pairs of twins, Castor and Pollux, Helen and Clytemnestra, hatched from one egg each (Euripides, *Helen*, 17–21).

Leonardo da Vinci had planned to paint a *Leda with the Swan* from about 1504 on. Two pen drawings of a kneeling Leda (Rotterdam, Chatsworth) have been preserved. They were the prototype for this Leda by Giampietrino (probably Gian Pietro Rizzi), a painter for whom there is no documentary evidence. In his composition, Giampietrino left out the swan, the instrument of seduction, and emphasised the elemental fecundity of female nature bringing forth four children. Leonardo's original pictorial invention has, nevertheless, influenced this one of about 1530/35.

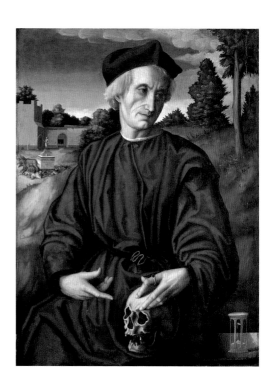

The plants and rocks in the foreground and the mountain landscape in the background may have been painted by the scarcely known Bernazzano, who also collaborated with other Leonardo pupils in this domain. *JML*

Francesco d'Ubertino, known as Il Bacchiacca

1494 Borgo S. Lorenzo – 1557 Florence

Portrait of Pope Hadrian VI as a Priest, about 1525
poplar wood panel, 98.2 x 73.3 cm –
GK 484

On the bench at the lower right is the inscription: NEC.QUE.PRETER-IIT.HORA.REDIRE.POTEST ("the hour that has passed cannot return").

Together with the attributes of the skull and hourglass and the representation of the 'triumph of death' in the background (after a Florentine print of the 15th century), the inscription refers to the death of the sitter. Adriaan Florensz. (1459–1523) was the only man from the Netherlands ever on the Papal throne. His role as the tutor of Charles V and regent of Spain (1520–1522) was historically more important than his term of office in the Apostolic See, which ended after little over a year in 1523. In response to the teachings of Martin Luther, he had planned a church reform that he was not able to implement. The death of this modest man was universally deplored. The Pope's posthumous portrait in priestly robes was made in 1525, soon after his death. The precise draughtsmanship and the heavy opaque paints are characteristic of the early Mannerist period in Rome and Florence. *JML*

Tiziano Vecellio, known as Titian

about 1488/90 Pieve di Cadore – 1576 Venice

Portrait of a Commander-in-Chief about 1550/55
canvas, 229 x 155.5 cm – GK 488

signed on the rock: TITIANVS/FECIT

The imposing life-sized figure of a military commander, his pose manifesting a Renaissance prince's claim to power, stands as the personification of the god of war, a 'new Mars,' in front of a broad river landscape. The brigandine covered with red velvet, the coat of mail, sword and dagger, lance, the red hat and the splendid dress helmet with a dragon crest indicate the high rank of the sitter, who is accompanied by his hound. The presence of little Amor, playing with the arms of Mars, elevates the fiercely glaring prince to the rank of an ancient god.

As Titian reserved full-sized portraits only for personalities of the highest rank (e.g. Emperor Charles V, King Philipp II of Spain, Pope Paul III), the sitter is likely to be closely connected to the emperor. It is probably a portrait of the Italian Prince Ferrante Gonzaga (1507–1557), a distinguished commander in many battles waged by Charles V, Viceroy of Sicily and governor in Milan and Lombardy. The son of Isabella d'Este and brother of Federico Gonzaga, the Duke of Mantua, Ferrante maintained relations with Titian, as they did, for many years.

This allegorical portrait of a ruler, with its impressionistic looking landscape in the background and expres-

sive colours, was painted about 1550/55. It is one of the most beautiful and outstanding portraits Titian ever made. *JML*

Jacopo Tintoretto

1518 Venice – 1594 Venice

Lot and his Daughters, about 1555
canvas, 116 x 147 cm – GK 1149
on loan from the Federal Republic of
Germany

After the destruction of the cities of Sodom and Gomorrah by fire and brimstone, only the pious Lot and his family were able to escape. Whereas his wife turned into a pillar of salt during the flight, Lot and his daughters made it to Zoar, where they lived in a cave. Because the daughters feared they would remain childless, they made

their father drunk with wine and slept with him without his noticing. Both became pregnant, the elder giving birth to Moab and the younger to Ammon, the ancestors of the Moabites and the Ammonites (Genesis 19: 30–38).

Tintoretto went to Rome in 1545 to study the sculptures and frescoes of Michelangelo. The motif of the seated Lot is clearly based on the figure of Isaiah on the ceiling fresco in the Sistine Chapel. In his painting of about 1555, the figures are placed diagonally on the picture plane. They appear to float, though they still have more physical volume than those in the artist's later works. The clothing and the still-life in the foreground are particularly attractive in their textures. Tintoretto's choice of colours is strongly influenced by his model Titian. *JML*

Francesco da Ponte, known as Bassano

1549 Bassano – 1592 Venice

Christ in the House of Martha and Mary, about 1576
canvas, 133 x 182.5 cm – GK 514

This painting is inscribed at the lower left on the pedestal of the column: (F)RANC.^{vs}/BASS.^{is}/FAC. It shows a domestic New Testament scene, the visit of Christ to the house of Martha and Mary in Bethany. Martha had invited Christ and his disciples to dine; while she was busy seeing to the preparations for the meal, Mary sat listening to the words of the Saviour. When Martha complained, Christ answered: "Mary hath chosen that good part" (Luke 10: 38–42).

Bassano uses the Biblical subject to depict a veritable kitchen still-life – the preparation of a large meal – with a number of details. In the foreground he spreads out a still-life consisting of fish, melon, and plucked fowl. On the right a maid is browning meat over a fire in the hearth; plates and pots on the walls identify the space as a kitchen, which opens up in the background to a dark landscape. Bread and wine on the table refer to the Last Supper, a common subject in Renaissance art.

JML

Jacopo Negretti, known as Palma il Giovane

1548 Venice – 1628 Venice

Venus in the Forge of Vulcan
about 1610
canvas 114.8 x 167.3 cm – GK 502

As described by the Roman poet Virgil in his *Aeneid*, Venus the goddess of love went to the forge of Vulcan, the god of the blacksmith's art, to ask him to make armour for her son Aeneas. Captivated by Venus's beauty, Vulcan forged divine arms that made Aeneas invincible. Vulcan's fee consisted of a night of love with the goddess.

Starting with Giorgione's *Reclining 'Venus* (Dresden), the subject of the nude women (*ignuda*) was varied in 16th-century Venetian painting by many artists. Paintings of the reclining Venus by Titian in Berlin and Florence were the point of departure for Palma's composition, which he drafted in several preliminary drawings. In these, Palma paid particular attention to the group of Vulcan and his apprentices in the background. Bright colours (red, blue, white) form the frame around the radiant beauty of the womanly, mature goddess of love. The new sense of physicality of the early Baroque replaces the floating Mannerist figures derived from Tintoretto that are characteristic of Palma's earlier works (e.g. *Christ Throwing the Merchants out of the Temple*, GK 1145). This Venus, created when the extremely prolific painter and draughtsman was about 60 years old, is one of his most magnificent works.   *JML*

**Giuseppe Cesari,
known as Cavaliere d'Arpino**
1568 Arpino – 1640 Rome

The Betrayal of Christ, about 1597
walnut panel, 88.5 x 62 cm – GK 598

While Jesus was praying on the Mount of Olives with his disciples at night, Judas led the high priest and his henchmen to Christ and betrayed him with a

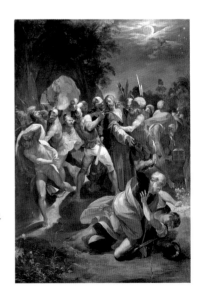

kiss. In the ensuing mayhem, Peter cut off the ear of Malchus, a servant of the high priest. Christ, however, healed the wounded man and let himself be led off without resistance (Mark 14: 43–53).

As early as the 17th century, Roman art historians (Bellori) counted this picture and a smaller second version in the Borghese Gallery among the most beautiful works by Cesari. The night scene was painted about 1596/97 in Rome, where the artist had been working for several cardinals and Pope Gregory XIII since 1582. The composition formed by complicated movements is typical for Roman Mannerism, as is the cold, almost piercing colour. In the group of Peter and Malchus the influence of graphic works by Dürer is evident. Until the arrival of Caravaggio and the Carraccis, Cesari was one of the leading painters in Rome; by the time he died in 1640 he had outlived not only his great competitors but also himself. *JML*

Michelangelo Cerquozzi
1602 Rome – 1660 Rome

Garden Party with a Group of Roman Artists, about 1640
canvas, 97.5 x 132.5 cm – GK 554

In his youth Cerquozzi had many contacts to Dutch artists in Rome (Paulus Bor, W. Michiels, and above all Pieter Van Laer, known as 'Bamboccio'). In the *Bambocciant* group with van Laer, Jan Miel, Karel Dujardin and others, he soon came to play an important role.

This is illustrated in his *Garden Party* painted about 1640, showing a merry company gathered for their artists' party. In the foreground six men sitting around a table are playing cards; on the left is the painter himself, having his pulse taken by a doctor. Other participants are a fellow painter in a white shirt up front, a dignified abbot and a richly dressed host on the right, as well as young women in splendid toilette, a second-hand vendor offering antiquities for sale, and blind man's bluff players in the background. Cerquozzi, a member of the Roman Accademia di S. Luca since 1634, often collaborated as a painter of figures with Viviano Codazzi and Gaspard Dughet; he also became known as a still-life painter. His major works include the *Revolt of Masaniello in Naples* of 1647, which came to a bloody end. It establishes the painter as a critical observer of contemporary political events. *JML*

Bernardo Cavallino
1616 Naples – 1656 Naples

Tobias Healing his Blind Father,
about 1640
canvas, 70 x 77.2 cm – GK 477

The apocryphal Book of Tobit (11:
13–15) tells the story of the young
Tobias travelling with Archangel
Raphael and catching a large fish in
the River Tigris. When he returns
home he uses the gall bladder of the
fish to anoint the blind eyes of his old
father Tobias (or Tobit), causing him
to regain his sight. In Cavallino's painting the miraculous cure is also wit-
nessed by Hannah and Sarah, the
bride of young Tobias, besides the
archangel.

Born in Naples, Cavallino learned
painting from Andrea Vaccaro and
Massimo Stanzione, two masters influenced by Caravaggio. As a young prod-
igy he was also open to the colour in-
novations of Rubens and van Dyck.
Thus he developed highly original refined chromatics in his canvases, where
cool colours such as light blue and
moss green combine with brown hues
and enamel white in unique harmo-
nies. The lyrically inclined painter
probably projected a cycle of scenes
from the story of Tobias, as copies in

other collections demonstrate. He was
thereby following a Baroque tradition
established by Domenico Fetti in
Mantua.   *JML*

**Alessandro Turchi,
known as l'Orbetto**
1578 Verona – 1649 Rome

Perseus Freeing Andromeda, about
1635
canvas, 111.5 x 138 cm – GK 543

Cassiopeia, the wife of the Egyptian
King Cepheus, had boasted that she
was more beautiful than the Nereids.
By way of punishment Poseidon sent a
sea monster. Cepheus had his daughter
Andromeda chained, the chains forged
to a rock, in order to sacrifice her to
the dragon. However, Perseus came
rushing over through the skies on Pegasus, the winged horse, killed the dragon and won the lovely Andromeda as
his wife. This dramatic event is described by the Roman poet Ovid in
his *Metamorphoses*, Book IV.

Alessandro Turchi was a pupil of Fe-
lice Brusasorzi in Verona before he
moved to Rome in 1614/15. There
he formed the 'trio dei Veronesi' with
his Veronese friends Pasquale Ottino
and Marcantonio Bassetti. Influenced

by the works of the Carraccis in Rome, the three artists developed a style that blended Classical and naturalistic elements. Turchi based his composition on the fresco in the Galleria Farnese in Rome executed by Annibale Carracci and Domenichino. The delicate tonal gradations of the clothes and the naturalistic details in this painting completed in the 1630s show Turchi to be an independent painter headed for the Roman high Baroque style. *JML*

Giulio Carpioni
1613 Venice – 1679 Vicenza

The Blind Seer Tiresias and
the Infant Narcissus, about 1650/60
canvas, 115 x 157 cm – GK 1158
on loan from the Federal Republic
of Germany

In the *Metamorphoses* (III, 339–350) the Roman poet Ovid tells of the birth of Narcissus, whose parents were Cephissus and the nymph Liriope. Not long after his birth, his mother brought the infant to the blind clairvoyant Tiresias and asked him whether her son would reach old age. The soothsayer's answer was: "Yes, if he remains a stranger to himself." The seer's words soon came true, when the youth saw himself mir-

rored in a spring. He fell in love with his reflection and, consumed with yearning for himself, died. The flowers named after Narcissus sprouted from the ground on the spot where he died.

Carpioni was the only Italian Baroque painter to deal repeatedly with this elegiac theme: other versions in Padua, Venice, Vienna suggest a lively humanistic interest among Carpioni's highly educated patrons in Vicenza and in northern Italy. Influenced by Titian and Poussin, Carpioni was a painter, draughtsman and engraver who was one of the most brilliant figures in Venetian art of the 17th century. *JML*

Antonio Bellucci
1654 Pieve di Soligo (Treviso) –
1726 Pieve di Soligo

Antiochus and Stratonice
(The Sick Prince), about 1700
canvas, 252.5 x 301 cm – GK 527

One of the favourite paintings of Johann Wolfgang von Goethe, who visited the Kassel gallery several times, is Bellucci's *Sick Prince*, which he described in his novel, *Wilhelm Meisters Lehrjahre*. The love story with a happy end has been handed down by Plutarch and Valerius Maximus: Antiochus I (324–261 BC), the son of Seleucus I, had fallen seriously ill due to his secret love for his young stepmother, Stratonice. The king's personal physician, Erasistratos, found out the cause of the disease while feeling the patient's pulse when Stratonice appeared. Thereupon Seleucus I generously relinquished his wife and let his son marry her.

Bellucci, who did a lot of work in European residences (Venice, Vienna, Düsseldorf, London, etc.) incorporated

influences from Paolo Veronese and Pietro da Cortona in his magnificently colourful paintings. He created a history painting with solemn dignity which was intended to decorate a (Venetian?) palace. *JML*

Giacomo Ceruti, known as il Pitocchetto
1698 Milan – 1767 Milan

Still-Life with Birds, Hare and Lobster, about 1736/38
canvas, 63 x 67.5 cm – GK 986

Between 1736 and 1738 Giacomo Ceruti painted a cycle of four still-lifes for Marshall Johann Matthias von der Schulenburg, who resided in Venice and had been in the services of the Venetian Republic since 1715. Both this still-life and another in an Italian private collection belong to this cycle.

Still-lifes are very rare in Ceruti's oeuvre. The socially critical Lombard realist was the subject of a large monographic exhibition in Bergamo in 1987. He made a name for himself with pictures of the everyday life of peasants and beggars in the area around Brescia (Lombardy) and with very realistic portraits. In this still-life he demonstrates his ability to use different modes of painting depending on

the object depicted. Thus the hare and the birds are in the style of the Flemish artist Jan Fyt (1611–1661), with all the details of the fur and the feathers precisely depicted. The application of the paint makes the lobster in the centre look hard and opaque. Other parts of the picture are painted more freely and flowingly. The effect of the principal colours is underscored by the way the objects are highlighted against the dark background.   *JML*

grow huge ass's ears because of his lack of understanding (*Metamorphoses* XI, 147–180).

In the centre of the picture Apollo reclines in the spotlight on drapery and plays his lyre. In front of him crouches Pan, and blows his panpipes. On the left is King Midas, already growing a pair of ass's ears. The main figures are surrounded by the muses, whose leader is Apollo. With its flickering light and dark, and its strongly contrasting colours, this painting of about 1720 is closely related to the works of G.B. Piazzetta and F. Bencovich. Damini settled in Acquila in the 1730s and completed a large number of altarpieces for the city's churches.

JML

Vincenzo Damini
about 1690/96 Venice – after 1749 Acquila (Abruzzi)

The Judgement of Midas, about 1720
canvas, 89.5 x 108 cm – GK 873

According to the Roman poet Ovid's account, Apollo, the god of light, and Pan, the cloven-footed god, competed with each other in a musical contest. The mountain god Tmolus declared Apollo, who played the lyre, the winner. The Phrygian King Midas, who appeared at the contest with his entourage, said the judgement of Tmolus was unfair. Thereupon Apollo had him

Giovanni Battista Piazzetta
1683 Venice – 1754 Venice

The Madonna Appearing to the Guardian Angel
canvas, 72.5 x 50 cm – GK 533

After studying art in Paris, Vouet travelled to Italy in 1612–13, first to Venice and then to Rome for a longer stay (until 1627). There he was influenced by Caravaggio, Manfredi and G. Honthorst, and later by Guido Reni as well. Vouet's half-length figures in this work painted in Rome show Sophonisba with the messenger clad in shiny armour, and a lamenting maid on the left. The light and dark contrasts derived from Caravaggio combine with ideals of beauty from Reni, to whom the painting was attributed up to the 18th century.   *JML*

Nicolas Poussin
1594 Villers, Normandy – 1665 Rome

Bacchic Scene
(Amor's Triumph over Pan),
about 1627
canvas, 96 x 74.5. cm – GK 459

The omnipresent power of Amor, the god of love, to whom both the mortals and the immortals are subject, is the theme of this work painted by Poussin in Rome around 1627. The cloven-hoofed shepherd god obeys Amor's command and takes Venus, the goddess of love, piggyback on his shoulders to carry her off. A winged cupid provides assistance and a faun with a basket of fruit follows the train, which is led by Amor, the winner, carrying Pan's staff and panpipes. The scene is set in a forest landscape flooded with golden light (Arcadia), which is closely related

to classical landscapes by the Carraccis. Poussin had also studied Titian's *Bacchanal*. In this cabinet-piece he follows the classical ideal, adding Neo-Classical elements in the composition of the figures and the rather cool colours. Poussin, renowned in Rome around 1630, was summoned to Paris in 1641 by Louis XIII as the court painter (*premier peintre du roi*). After returning to Rome in 1642, he remained active there until his death. *JML*

Sébastien Bourdon

1616 Montpellier – 1671 Paris

Soldiers Playing Cards
in a Camp, 1643
oak panel, 36.5 x 50 cm – GK 471

The painting is inscribed on a tablet at the upper left of the pillar: "bon vyn/1643." It shows a very realistic scene from the Thirty Years' War: soldiers resting in an improvised temporary camp. The sutler nursing her baby in the right foreground is the focal point in the group. A young girl pours wine for her from a jug; three card-players gathered around a barrel keep her company. Even the soldier just dismounted from his horse in front of the tent in the left middle ground is doing justice to the wine.

Bourdon left France for Rome in 1634, where he frequented the *Bamboccianti* circle of friends and artists with Pieter van Laer and Michelangelo Cerquozzi. Pieter van Laer (1599–1642) was also the source of the theme of *Resting in a Camp* and of several of the figures' poses. He also followed the Haarlem painter closely in the delicate blending of the technique. In 1648 Bourdon was one of the founding fathers of the Académie Royale de Peinture in Paris. Because of his outstanding talent, which also tempted him to paint fakes, he was highly regarded as a painter and art theorist. *JML*

Flora Room

Adriaen van der Werff

1659 Kralingen – 1722 Rotterdam

Flora with Putti Scattering
Flowers, 1696
canvas, 290 x 194 cm – GK 315

The influence of French culture in late
17th-century Holland enhanced interior decoration according to the tenets
of Neo-Classicism, which included
making use of painting. The major example dating from the end of the century is a ten-part cycle Adriaen van der
Werff painted to decorate the garden
salon of his own home in Rotterdam.
The six paintings that have been preserved are displayed in the newly set
up Flora Room here. They include the
famous *Shepherd in Love* and three ceiling paintings of flowers and fruits symbolising springtime and fertility. In the
central painting on the ceiling, between foliate masks and acanthus gar-

lands, a round opening exposes the sky. Floating across it is the flower goddess Flora with a floral wreath and cupids scattering blossoms The figures and ornament of this kind of art combine carefree charm and precise order. It was inspired mainly by the distinguished French ornamental designer Daniel Marot, who had emigrated to The Hague for religious reasons in 1685. *BS*

Jacob de Wit
1696 Amsterdam – 1754 Amsterdam

Allegory of Autumn, 1752
inscr. lower right: J.dWit 1752
canvas, 216 x 145.5 cm – GK 433

The first building to house the gallery in Kassel, constructed from 1749 to 1751, had two doors at each of the narrow ends. For the overdoors, Landgrave Wilhelm VIII commissioned four allegories of the seasons from the famous Amsterdam decorator, Jacob de

Wit. They were delivered in 1751 and 1752. Painted in pale shades of grey, they imitate stone reliefs, a technique that was centuries old and still effective in the 18th century. "I have heard that a piece by de Wit has arrived in Kassel that is supposed to look like marble," Baron Häckel wrote from Frankfurt to his friend Wilhelm VIII. In traditional symbolic language, Bacchus personifies the autumn along with the pine-cone-topped *thyrsus* (staff), vine leaves, grapes, jug and picher. Despite the Rococo-like playfulness of the scene with cupids, the composition of a stele with a bust in the central axis of an arched niche is architecturally severe. *BS*

Johann Heinrich Tischbein the Elder
1722 Haina/Hesse – 1789 Kassel

The Mocking of Anacreon, 1754
canvas, 165 x 113 cm – GK 1212

After refining his art studies in France and Italy, Tischbein was engaged by Wilhelm VIII in 1754 as court painter in Kassel. This was when *The Mocking of Anacreon* and the companion-piece showing *Hercules and Omphale* (GK 1211) were painted as commissions from the landgrave. Although he usually had Tischbein decorate his palaces, both history paintings were given a place of honour among the masterpieces filling Wilhelm VIII's art gallery. The two paintings are linked by the common theme of a couple in classical antiquity, formed with Amor's help, consisting of a mature man and a young seductress with the latter taking advantage of her admirer's being madly in love in order to make a fool of him.

While Omphale has Hercules wear women's clothing, the aged Anacreon must put up with being lured by his adored one in a revealing dress, only to be brusquely rejected in the end just before achieving his goal. Anacreon lived in the 6th century BC in Ionia and wrote verses that focus mainly on love and wine. There is no evidence in the picture to support an earlier identification of the woman with the poetess Sappho.   *HJC*

Giuseppe Nogari
1699 Venice – 1766 Venice

Painting and Sculpture,
about 1751
canvas, 142.5 x 113.5 cm – GK 537

Giuseppe Nogari was an apprentice of Giovanni Battista Piazzetta in Venice,

who taught Johann Heinrich Tischbein the Elder as well. Landgrave Wilhelm VIII presumably became acquainted with works by this Venetian painter, who was already highly renowned by the middle of the 18th

century, through his advisor Baron von Häckel. It was also through Häckel's mediation that purchasing an allegorical pair of paintings directly from Nogari for the landgrave's collection succeeded in 1751. One of these two is devoted to the fine arts, painting and sculpture. Deep in conversation, the personifications of the sister arts are shown as two charming girls with the characteristic implements and attributes of their respective arts. Interestingly enough, Nogari positioned sculpture slightly lower than her sister, thus expressing a claim to superiority for his own profession. The companion-piece (GK 538) shows the arts of music and poetry in mirrored symmetry. *HJC*

Johann Melchior Roos
1663 Heidelberg –
1731 (?) Brunswick (?)

The Menagerie of
Landgrave Karl, 1721–1728
canvas, 339 x 671 cm – GK 1114

The princely passion for collecting exotic animals has been documented for the Hessian landgraves back to the

15th century. Under Landgraves Karl and Friedrich II, Kassel had two large menageries, located in the Karlsaue not far from the Orangerie. Landgrave Karl's zoo is first mentioned in 1688. It included bears, lions, tigers, dromedaries, ostriches, peacocks, parrots, monkeys, porcupines, a civet and a lynx. These and other animals, as well as a pug are depicted in this enormous painting commissioned by Karl from the animal painter J.M. Roos in 1721. It was not completed until 1728. Exhibited in the Kunsthaus, it was considered a sensation up to the end of the century, for which there is considerable evidence. After spending 60 years in storage, it has now been painstakingly restored thanks to the financial support of private patrons in Kassel. The composition adapts Netherlandish models such as *Adam and Eve among the Animals in Paradise* or *Orpheus Charming the Animals* (Roelant Savery, Jan van Kessel), reducing their themes to a pure animal study. *BS*

Johann Liss

about 1597 Oldenburg, Holstein –
1631 Verona

The Morra Game, about 1621
canvas, 75.3 x 55.9 cm – GK 186

Out of doors in an arbour, seven
young people are playing the so-called
game of *morra* (or *mora*), which had
been common in Italy since antiquity.
Like odds and evens, each player shows
one or more fingers of one hand at a
given moment; whoever named the
correct number beforehand, wins the
game. Two figures particularly stand
out: the splendidly dressed gentleman
in the foreground, in red breeches and
with coloured feathers in his hat, and
the beauty dressed in white and blue,
who is looking up at him. In their case
the game of chance is joined by the
game of love. Other erotic references
include the young man picking grapes
and his lute-playing partner ("If music
be the food of love..."), the barking
dog and the pair of birds on the perch.

Johann Liss, the most important
German painter of the early Baroque
period, took to the road from about
1615 on, journeying via Amsterdam
and Paris to Venice and Rome. This is
where the painter, who died young,
created his masterpieces, including
scenes from everyday life influenced
by Caravaggio and the Venetian masters. In his *Morra Game*, which is
flooded with light, Liss anticipates the
spirit of the Rococo.   *JML*

Ignaz Stern, known as Stella
1679 Mauerkirchen – 1748 Rome

Spring, about 1723–24
canvas, 149.5 x 103.5 cm – GK 1065
Gift of B. Braun Melsungen AG, 1990

Since 1990, the Kassel gallery has exhibited the complete cycle of the *Four Seasons* by Ignaz Stern, which joined the collection in the 1980s as a gift of the B. Braun Company of Melsungen. With works by Johann Liss and Johann Carl Loth, they now form an ensemble representing the German Baroque painters who worked in Italy. The most splendid picture of the cycle of the *Seasons* is *Spring*. Flora, the youthful goddess of the flowers is shown here with a winged cupid (Amor) as Primavera (spring), the first season. Representing the corresponding sign of the zodiac, the ram (Aries) is contentedly chewing a flower from a basket filled with spring flowers. This delicately painted still-life and the luxuriant vegetation in the background celebrate the rebirth of nature, youth and beauty. Together with the paintings of *Summer*, *Autumn* and *Winter*, the *Spring* forms a high point in the work of the painter, who worked in Bologna, Forli and primarily in Rome. Permeated with the joyful spirit of Rococo, his works were praised by his contemporaries for their "grazia e delicatezza," which can be traced directly to Correggio and Parmigianino.   *JML*

Johann Heinrich Schönfeld
1609 Biberach a.d. Riss –
1684 Augsburg

The Great Flood, about 1636/37
canvas, 137.5 x 208 cm – GK 918

According to the account in the Bible (Genesis 6:7), God decided in view of

the sinful doings of mankind, to wipe all people and animals off the face of the earth by letting it rain for forty days and forty nights. Only the righteous Noah and his family, with one pair each of all the animals, were able to escape in the Ark, where they were the only ones to survive. High mountains frame the turbulent sea in which people of all ages are trying to rescue themselves; drowning men and women shown in daring foreshortened poses are scattered across the foreground. Only a few, such as the woman lamenting the death of her child and the man on the raft, are still alive. Above them and above all the other figures, heavy rain pours from dense grey-blue clouds, meaning the end for everyone. In the background, Noah's Ark is battling the elements. After staying in Stuttgart and Basel, Schönfeld worked from 1633 to 1648 in Rome and Naples. This is also where *The Great Flood* was painted under the influence of painters such as Antonio Carracci and Nicolas Poussin.

The mellowness of its colours shows up especially in the foreground details. Schönfeld, who settled in Augsburg in 1651, created altarpieces for the local cathedral and other churches in southern Germany. Joachim von Sandrart extolled the "uncommon grace" of the works by this major Baroque painter. *JML*

Jan van Nikkelen
1656 Haarlem – 1721 Kassel

View of the Grottoes and the Octagon with the Pyramid and the Statue of Hercules atop the Habichtswald 1716
canvas, 169 x 149 cm – GK 1099

In 1716 Landgrave Karl commissioned from the Dutch architectural painter a cycle of eight ideal landscape views of the palace and gardens on the eastern slope of the wood called Habichtswald. The artist worked on them until just before his death. The views of the grounds expand step by step, showing

the palaces, grottoes, fountains and terrace gardens, ending in a perspective of the entire design, which was to begin at the foot of the slope. When the vast project designed by Giovanni Guerniero was realised in 1701–1718, the landgrave had to make do with the upper third only. The painted views were to compensate for the incomplete grounds, enhancing them with additional details. The painting exhibited, number one of this unique architectural series, is a close-up of Kassel's landmark above Wilhelmshöhe Palace. With the coloured stucco of the architecture, flanked by two small temples that were never built, the structure surmounted by the virtuous hero Hercules looks more cheerful and light than it does in reality.   *BS*

Connecting Tract

Januarius Zick
1730 Munich – 1797 Ehrenbreitstein

The Circumcision of Christ, after 1751
canvas, 55.5 x 79 cm – GK 1140

Rembrandt's paintings and etchings served as a source of inspiration for many later painters, who incorporated mainly the Amsterdam master's compositional inventions into their works long into the 18th century.

Zick's painting testifies to this influence. For the arrangement of the group of figures on the left the southern German artist chose an early etching of the Circumcision by Rembrandt (Bartsch 48) as his point of departure. In combination with other borrowings in the figures and colours from the works of Tintoretto, Zick created a new whole that demonstratively picks up the pictorial inventions of his forerunners and, by combining them, tries to assimilate them and even to improve on them.

The subject matter is provided by the account of the evangelist St Luke: "And after eight days were accomplished, that the child should be circumcised, his name was called Jesus, which was called by the angel, before he was conceived in the womb." (2:21)   *HJC*

Johann Georg Platzer
1704 St Michael in Eppan, South Tyrol –
1761 St Michael in Eppan

The Marriage of Bacchus and
Ariadne in Naxos, about 1740
inscr. lower left: J:g.plazer
copper, 40.8 x 60 cm – GK 646

The Battle of the Centaurs and Lapiths
at the Wedding Feast of Peirithous and
Hippodamia (companion-piece of
GK 646), about 1740
copper, 40.8 x 60 cm – GK 647

In these two small cabinet-pieces Platzer illustrates two stories from classical
mythology, namely two wedding feasts
that came to very different ends. In the
first picture Bacchus, the god of wine,
is celebrating his marriage to Ariadne,
the daughter of the Cretan King
Minos, at a sumptuous feast on the island of Naxos. She had been aban-
doned on the island by her fiancé Theseus, who had rescued her from the
labyrinth. Bacchus had come and
comforted her in her sorrow. Dancing
and making music, the entourage of
the god of wine are celebrating the
event in an extended mountainous
landscape. By contrast, there is a highly
dramatic finale to the wedding feast of
Peirithous, the king of the Lapiths, and
Hippodamia, the daughter of the Ar-
give hero Adrastos. Among the guests,
the Centaurs, hybrid creatures half
man and half horse, were soon drunk
and molested the bride and the wives
of the Lapiths. The result was a fierce

battle in the banqueting hall of the palace. Shown in the centre is the attempt of a Centaur to ravish the bride. The furnishings of the palace are depicted in minute detail.

Platzer had first been a pupil of his uncle Christoph Platzer in Passau. He became a member of the Viennese Academy of Art in 1728, and from 1730 to 1755 he was one of the most highly esteemed masters of Viennese Rococo oriented on Dutch 17th-century painting.   JML

Johann Rudolf Byss

1662 Chur, Switzerland – 1738 Würzburg

Flower Still-Life with Blue Tit, 1702
inscr. lower centre: J.R.Bijs.fe:Ao.1702
oak panel, 50 x 34.3 cm – GK 909

Standing on a ledge is a twisted glass vase with a bunch of flowers that fills up almost the entire picture plane. The lavish bouquet contains irises, tulips and narcissus, roses and hyacinths, morning glories and cowslips; a hydrangea completes the arrangement. A blue tit sitting under it on the left looks out at the viewer.

Having studied with his father in Solothurn, Byss travelled in England and Holland as well as Italy in the 1680s. From 1689 he worked in Prague for the Counts Czernin. From 1713 to 1738 he worked in various capacities in Bamberg, Pommersfelden and finally as an interior architect at the residence in Würzburg. His flower still-life of 1702 painted in the style of Roelant Savery (1576–1639), i.e. in the style of an 'old master,' was made to complete a still-life by this Dutch painter, which is now preserved in the Liechtenstein Gallery in Vaduz.   JML

Johann Heinrich Tischbein the Elder

1722 Haina, Hesse – 1789 Kassel

Jupiter and Callisto, 1756
inscr. lower left: JHTischbein Pinx 1756
canvas, 41 x 47 cm – GK 690

Acis and Galatea, 1758
inscr. lower left: JHTischbein Pinx 1758
canvas, 40.8 x 47 cm – GK 691

The prestigious Kassel court painter knew perfectly how to adapt to different projects. The present pair of companion-pieces, which Tischbein painted for the private palace of the prince, differ from the two large gallery paintings exhibited in the Flora Room not only in their small size and hence the more detailed technique but also in their subject matter. Contrasting with the hero Hercules and the poet Anacreon, figures with a broad range of action, these two nymphs play a role in Ovid's *Metamorphoses* only because of their beauty and their fateful love. One is a passive and the other an active lover. Both stories end tragically. Callisto, a shy nymph in Diana's entourage, is seduced by Jupiter disguised in the form of the goddess of the hunt. When her mistress discovers her pregnancy, she transforms her into a bear.

Galatea rejects the intense wooing of the giant Polyphemus and falls in love with the attractive Acis. The hulking one-eyed (three-eyed in Tischbein's case) giant spies on the lovers. In a jealous rage he rushes out and kills Acis with a huge rock as he escapes towards the sea.

Since Rubens's famous painting of *Jupiter and Callisto* of 1613, the story had been depicted as a masterly performance of ingratiating seduction. Tischbein follows this example, which was already in Kassel at the time, quite closely in the composition of the figures and Jupiter's caressing gestures. The Rococo-like, daintily elegant idiom of his forms thus distinguishes him all the more obviously from Rubens.   *BS*

Johann Heinrich Tischbein the Elder

1722 Haina, Hesse – 1789 Kassel

Landgrave Wilhelm VIII of Hesse-Kassel, about 1754–60
canvas, 38 x 32.5 cm – GK 1213

By painting a striking half-figure portrait of Wilhelm VIII as a military commander, which is now in the Schloss Fasanerie near Fulda, Tischbein had won the favour of this par-

in the small picture. These include the column with drapery, the palace interior, the ermine-lined mantle over the chair, the helmet and the prince's hat on the table, the commander's staff and the Polish Order of the White Eagle that Wilhelm always wore for official portraits. The sketchy figure in the upper right background with her arms around an obelisk is an allegory of princely fame or, in view of the feathered helmet, the goddess Minerva, guardian of the arts. Her presence sheds light on the role Wilhelm VIII assumed in his old age.   *BS*

ticularly critical patron in 1753. Not long after his appointment as the court painter, he painted the present study for a full-length portrait. It was only carried out as a half-figure portrait, however, possibly because the remarkably squat figure did not appeal to the prince. All the elements of an official state portrait have been sketched out

Justus Juncker

1702/03 Mainz – 1767 Frankfurt am Main

The Master at his Easel, 1752
inscr. left centre: Juncker fecit 1752
oak panel, 48 x 36.8 cm – GK 641

In the 16th and 17th centuries, Italian and particularly Dutch painters had painted numerous interiors of artists' studios, often including a self-portrait. Juncker's 18th-century painting deliberately refers to this tradition. The famous artist presents himself sitting in front of his easel with his palette and brushes. On his right, a young pupil, under the critical gaze of his teacher, is drawing a plaster cast of a classical sculpture. Unlike the earlier studio scenes, however, Juncker's room hardly makes the impression of a workshop any more, but that of an orderly living room or study. In this way Juncker indicates that he wants to be seen less as a craftsman and more as a *pictor doctus*, a learned artist, whose work is to be rated primarily as an intellectual activity. In addition, the numerous paintings on the walls indicate that, besides having a productive role, he also has that of a knowledgeable collector and art lover, who, moreover, takes the trouble to provide the younger generation with proper training. *HJC*

spade in art. When she recognises the master and throws herself at his feet, he speaks the words of the Gospel of St John written in Latin along the hem of his robe: "Do not touch me, for I am not yet ascended to my Father." The days of familiar togetherness with Jesus are over. In the middle- and background are four other scenes from the story of the Resurrection: the two Maries at the empty tomb, the encounter between Jesus and the three Maries, and the meeting of the pilgrims to Emmaus as well as the supper at Emmaus. The painting, which is enhanced by many plants and a mountain landscape with a distant view conforming to late Gothic formal concepts, is in exceptionally well preserved condition. It is the earliest painting preserved by this artist; the date of 1507 in Roman numerals appears on the ointment jar. *BS*

Second Floor

Jacob Cornelisz.
van Oostsanen
about 1472 Oostsanen –
1533 Amsterdam

Christ with Mary Magdalen, 1507
oak panel, 54.5 x 38.8 cm – GK 29

Mary Magdalen mistook the risen Christ for a gardener at first. He is therefore usually equipped with a

Joos van Cleve

1480/85 Kleve (?) – 1540/41 Antwerp

A Pair of Portraits of a Couple,
1525; 1526
oak panel, 64 x 49 cm each – GK 20;
GK 21

The numbers in the upper corners
of the two panels indicate that the
man was painted in 1526 at the age of
36 and the woman in 1525 at 38. The
half-length portraits presumably por-
tray members of the well-to-do middle class of Antwerp, as indicated by
their unpretentious but expensive
clothing and jewellery. The man
clutches his gloves firmly in his right
hand, while the woman moves the
beads of her rosary around with fingers
covered with several rings. The portraits are typical examples of the fully
developed Renaissance style of this
master. In comparison to the male
portraits by van Cleve of 1509 (L
1104) and about 1520 (GK 26) displayed nearby, the format has been increased to life-size and the physical

presence heightened by sculptural emphasis and self-confident facial expressions.   BS

Maerten van Heemskerck

1498 Heemskerck near Alkmaar –
1574 Haarlem

Pieter Jan Foppeszoon and his Family,
about 1530
oak panel, 118.7 x 140.2 cm – GK 33

The coat of arms on the signet ring in
the centre of the picture makes it possible to identify the educated Haarlem
burgher, who was known to be a
friend and patron of the young painter. Heemskerck created a family portrait for him that is unique in contemporary Dutch painting for its wealth of
detail and lifelike impression. The
viewer sees Jan Fopsen, his wife, and
his children having a meal, apparently
informally and realistically. However,
the representation is determined by
religious symbolism. The expressive
cloudy sky replacing the back wall of a

room removes the group with the happy children from everyday life. The glass of wine raised by the father of the house and the bread lying beside it refer to the Eucharist. The fruits and foods on the colourfully set table – one of the major precursors of still-life painting of the early 17th century – recall the Fall of Man (apple), the Crucifixion (nuts) and hope for life everlasting (cherries). The cheese, Lenten fare, symbolises the virtue of moderation. The obviously nude boy in the woman's arms grabbing the rosary has been convincingly interpreted as the Christ Child. This brings the example of the Holy Family into play. The pose of the mother and child can be compared to the Madonna in the painting by Heemskerck's teacher Jan van Scorel which is exhibited near by. *BS*

Frans Floris
1519/20 Antwerp – 1570 Antwerp

The Judgement of Paris,
about 1548
oak panel, 120 x 159.5 cm – GK 1001

In his legends about the heroes (*Heroides* 5, 16), the Roman writer Ovid tells the story of the dispute among the goddesses Hera, Athena and Aphrodite over the golden apple of Eris, the goddess of discord. This had been inscribed "for the fairest." The messenger of the gods, Hermes, leads the goddesses to Mount Ida, where the shepherd Paris is to pronounce judgement. Hera promised him the dominion over all of Asia, Athena victory in battle, Aphrodite the most beautiful of all mortal women. Desiring the beautiful Helen as his wife, Paris chose the goddess of love, Aphrodite. During his stay in Italy from 1541 to 1547, Floris

became familiar with the works of Raphael in Rome and the mythological frescoes by Giulio Romano in Mantua. Inspired by these, in about 1548 after his return to Antwerp he painted the *Judgement of Paris* with its splendid colours and the main characters in the foreground of a mountain landscape. The Classical sarcophagus and the figure of the river god Scamander are based on Roman prototypes. As Romanism's main representative, Floris propagated the Italian Renaissance ideal in the Low Countries.   *JML*

a commander of the imperial army of Charles V. The emperor had conferred this office upon the 22-year-old prince of Orange, whom he greatly favoured at the time, in July 1555. A cartouche within the golden ornamental ribbon on the breastplate shows exactly this year. Mor portrayed William I in a portrait form that had been customary for centuries. It was, moreover, lastingly affected by his inventions. It attempts to express the virtue and dignity of the ideal prince in his face and bearing. The German inscription is a

Anthonis Mor

1516/19 Utrecht – 1575/76 Antwerp

William I of Orange,
about 1555
oak panel, 105 x 82.1 cm – GK 37

Between 1560 and 1584, the year of his assassination, William I, known as The Silent, was the leader of the northern provinces' struggle for independence from Spain. The portrait shows him a few years before the outbreak of the conflict in the armour of

later addition, probably added as early as the 16th century. It addresses the sitter with the title of Count of Nassau-Katzenelnbogen and presumably documents hereditary claims of the house of Nassau to the wealthy county of Katzenelnbogen. *HJC*

Joachim Beuckelaer
about 1534 Antwerp –
about 1574 Antwerp

Market Scene, 1564
oak panel, 114.8 x 170.5 cm – GK 41

As in many other kitchen and market scenes by Beuckelaer, overflowing baskets, bowls and jugs with various kinds of fruits and vegetables are piled high facing the viewer. They are the wares of a market vendor, who, moreover, is proffering a duck in her hands. The entire presentation is made up of fruits from different seasons and reflects the abundance of nature as well as the related sensual delights of man. That it refers not only to food but also to the satisfaction of sexual desires is revealed by an awareness of the erotic connotations associated with many of the fruits and vegetables

as well as poultry that are depicted. In addition, the overwhelming opulence of the display includes a warning against the vice of immoderation. The painting, dated on the upper left, entered the collection of Landgrave Wilhelm VIII ascribed incorrectly to Beuckelaer's teacher Pieter Aertsen. *HJC*

Gonzales Coques
1618 Antwerp – 1684 Antwerp

The Young Scholar and his Wife, 1640
inscr. lower left: Gonsales F. 1640
oak panel, 41 x 59.5 cm – GK 151

This painter specialised in small portraits of couples or groups. The Kassel gallery possesses two early works. Of these, the one presented here is probably the most famous painting of all by this artist because of its refined technique, the natural dignity of the figures, and the charming interior. A prosperous young couple is in their sitting room, its walls decorated with gold-tooled leather and a frieze of landscape paintings. The man and woman each have their own sphere

of activity. He is perhaps a doctor, and is leafing with lecturing gestures through a book. On the table beside him are an anatomical figure with exposed muscles, an hourglass and a globe. She strikes the chord of marital harmony on the harpsichord. The instrument probably has more than a symbolic significance, for the depiction of *Midas's Judgement* inside the lid suggests her musical ambitions. The little dog on the chair is a traditional symbol of marital fidelity.　BS

Pieter Claesz.

1597/98 Burgsteinfurt –
1600/61 Haarlem

Breakfast Piece with Oysters
about 1630–35
inscr. lower left: PC (in monogram) /
16.3 (?)
oak panel, 37.8 x 53.2 cm – GK 437

The fixings for a small, but certainly fancy meal are shown as though in a snapshot. Bread, oysters, hazelnuts, a

lemon and a little tapering bag of pepper are in readiness to satisfy the appetite. The thirst can be quenched with the contents of a half-filled Roemer wineglass. In addition, a tazza bowl, an upside-down Berkemeyer glass, a silver plate and a knife are ready for use.

Apparently assembled by chance, this turns out to be a thoroughly planned pictorial arrangement. The descending order of the objects from left to right, the many overlapping forms and the perspective foreshortening allow the painter to display all of his expertise. Even the colouring is sensitively worked out, ranging mainly within a limited palette of brown and grey hues. This colour scheme makes the

picture belong to the group of still-lifes known as *monochrome banketjes* that were extremely popular in the northern Low Countries around 1620–40. *HJC*

Willem van Aelst

1625/26 Delft (?) –
after 1683 Amsterdam

Flower Still-Life with a
Pocket Watch, 1656
inscr. lower centre: W.V.aelst. 1656
canvas, 55 x 46.3 cm – GK 905

The floral arrangement is one of the oldest and most popular motifs in modern still-life painting. Willem van Aelst caused the genre to reach a peak of its development. The present painting is impressive not only for the brilliant depiction of roses, chrysanthemums and mallows but also for the depth of its pictorial space. The effect derives from the highlighting in combination with the twisted diagonal of the composition, starting with the blue watch ribbon in the front and reaching back via the rose to the mal-

low bud at the top. Van Aelst himself introduced this diagonal kind of a composition into flower still-life painting around the middle of the 17th century and it enjoyed enduring success. The pocket watch and the eaten-away leaves add a deeper meaning through their symbolic reference to the transitoriness of all earthly splendours. *HJC*

Gerard de Lairesse

1640 Liège – 1711 Amsterdam

Portrait of Philip de Flines, 1682
inscr.: G.Lairesse f ano 1682
canvas, 141 x 115 cm – GK 461

After his studies in the French-influenced Liège, the artist moved to Amsterdam in 1665. As a painter and art theorist he became a leading representative of academic Neo-Classicism, which had largely been rejected by Dutch painting to date, and he particularly dissociated himself from Rembrandt. Until he became blind in 1690, which limited his activity to lecturing, Lairesse almost exclusively painted scenes from mythology, ancient history and the Bible. This portrait is one of the few exceptions. The sitter played an important role for the artist. He was one of his major patrons and a driving force behind the artists' society *Nil volentibus arduum* (nothing is impossible for those who desire), which propagated Lairesse's ideas. Philip de Flines, a prosperous silk merchant, is shown in an elegant brown silk kimono, a fashionable piece of clothing that he had probably imported from Japan himself. The compass he holds on the map of Amsterdam represents his

cosmopolitanism in connection with foreign trade and his feeling of pride in his hometown.   BS

Godfried Schalken

1643 Made near Dordrecht –
1706 The Hague

Venus Attended by Amor;
Venus Hands Amor a Burning
Arrow, 1690
both inscr. lower left: G. Schalcken
canvas, 70.5 x 53 cm each – GK 306;
GK 307

In 1751 the Dutch art dealer Hoet acquired two companion-pieces with representations of Venus and Amor for Landgrave Wilhelm VIII. Their creator is the Dordrecht painter Godfried Schalcken, who was lauded in collec-

tions of biographies of artists as early as the 18th century as a master of precisely detailed brushwork and above all of the treatment of light. These two paintings, dated on the reverse, certain-

Jan Weenix
about 1642 Amsterdam –
1719 Amsterdam

Italian Seaport, about 1666
inscr. lower left: J. Weenix.
canvas, 115 x 158.5 cm – GK 1003

ly demonstrate Schalcken's extraordinary ability to depict complicated lighting conditions. Moreover, he does so in programmatic form. Besides their respective mythological events, the two masterpieces of this painter contrast different lighting effects, created in one case by the daylight and in the other by the artificial light of a flame. The model for the head of Venus in each case was Schalcken's wife, Françoise van Diemen.　*HJC*

Jan Weenix began his career with Italianate views of ports, a genre picked up from his father Jan Baptist Weenix. The arbitrary, completely unrealistic combination of ancient structures and Mediterranean coastal views, port scenes and all kinds of figures is characteristic. Caprice-like arrangements of motifs of this kind satisfied the Italy craze of large segments of the Dutch public in the 17th century. One motif in this painting that indicates Jan Weenix's authorship in particular is the still-life of dead game incorporated on the right beside the seated couple in the foreground. In the course of his development the artist came to focus increasingly on this variant of the still-life and became one of the painters of game still-lifes most in demand in Europe.　*HJC*

Adriaen van de Velde

1636 Amsterdam – 1672 Amsterdam

The Beach at Scheveningen, 1658
inscr. lower left: A. v. velde f 1658
canvas, 52.6 x 73.8 cm – GK 374

Adriaen van de Velde, scion of a remarkable dynasty of artists, was
equally talented as a landscapist and
figure painter. This also shows in his
five famous coastal landscapes, of
which this is the earliest and the most
highly regarded. The beach of the
fishing village of Scheveningen was
already a favourite site for outings for
the residents of nearby The Hague in
the 17th century. We can see them
relax on the damp sand, walking
through puddles with their clothes
hitched up and watching the activities of the fishermen as well as riding.
The main figure is the young man in
the right foreground, looking out to
sea with his hands behind his back.
This figure embodies the feeling of
carefree calm that overlies the sunny
morning scene (the shadows are
pointing westward). The depiction of
nature is very precise and poetically
transfigured at the same time. In the
reflections of the light and the shadows of the clouds on the water and
sand, the painter almost attains Impressionistic effects.   *BS*

Simon de Vlieger

about 1601 Rotterdam (?) – 1653 Weesp

Marine, about 1640
inscr. lower right: S DE VLIEGER
oak panel, 85.5 x 114.4 cm – GK 418

The artist had many talents but was
mainly known as a marine painter. In
this sizeable painting he shows a wide
estuary with a low horizon and high
skies. The clouds and the water are
stirred up by a strong wind; the sun
and the rain come together. The coast,
with many small ships before it, can
hardly be distinguished. The painter
uses a few carefully placed ships to

create depth in this great expanse: a fishing boat in the left foreground, a three-master in the middle ground, and a ship at anchor on the left again but in the far distance. He moves the viewer's eye through the space by changing the light: the boat is dark against flashing waves; the sails of the big vessel, touched by a ray of sunshine, are white against black clouds. The painterly appeal of bad weather as seen here was discovered and explored in Dutch landscape painting especially between 1625 and 1640.   BS

Salomon van Ruysdael
1600/03 Naarden – 1670 Haarlem

Estuary with Boats, about 1660
inscr. left on the canvas roof: SVR
(monogram)
oak panel, 37.3 x 55.3 cm – GK 396a

The broad Dutch landscape forms the motif dominating almost the entire oeuvre of Salomon van Ruysdael. Views of rivers constitute an especially large group of works. This painting is one of the late versions of these. Presented in the usual fashion, a wide estuary is spread out before the viewer, with plain inland boats, so-called 'Leichter' following their course and fishermen hauling in their nets on its calm waters. The silhouette of a town arises in the distance on the low horizon. The high sky with its fluffy clouds and the subdued evening light underscore the prevailing ambience of harmony, as does the restrained colour scheme that joins the zone of the sky and the surfaces of the water into an overall whole full of atmosphere.   HJC

Pieter Jansz. Saenredam
1597 Assendelft – 1665 Haarlem

The Interior of the Church of
St Mary, Utrecht, 1637
inscr. lower left: A.1637 / Saenredam. fecit
oak panel, 40 x 49.8 cm – GK 427

This painting entered the landgrave's collection as a Protestant counterpart

to the interior of a Catholic cathedral in 1738. It gives us an impression of the Romanesque Mariakerk in Utrecht, which no longer exists today. The view extends from the north side aisle through the nave and into the south transept, and is framed within the picture by the half columns and arches of the arcades in the foreground. Saenredam prepared his paintings with their carefully wrought perspectives and precise architectural details by making preparatory drawings on the premises. The study for this painting was drawn in June 1636 during the artist's five-month stay at the home of an acquaintance right opposite the Mariakerk. The signature and date appear below the medieval fresco of the Madonna on the wall panel on the far left. *HJC*

Paulus Potter

1625 Enkhuizen – 1654 Amsterdam

A Farmer with his Herd, 1648

inscr. lower right: Paulus Potter.f. 1648
oak panel, 50 x 74.5 cm – GK 369

This picture shows nothing but the flat Dutch landscape behind the dunes, with a farmhouse and a few trees, four cows, three sheep and a man between them, all in motionless tranquillity. In order to understand such a simple motif one must realise that the Dutch were very proud of the fertility of their marshland and their abundance of cattle; the cow even became their national symbol.

Paulus Potter, probably the most famous Dutch animal painter, succeeds in capturing the humid and mild sunny atmosphere of this land by the sea with a very subtle, detailed technique in warm light hues. A recent restoration has recaptured much of the original freshness of the colours. *BS*

Caspar Netscher
about 1636 Heidelberg (?) –
1684 The Hague

A Masquerade Joke, 1668
inscr. lower right: CNetscher f. 1668.
oak panel, 47 x 63.5 cm – GK 292

Landgrave Wilhelm VIII purchased
this genre scene in The Hague in 1752
as a technically particularly brilliant
work by Netscher, a pupil of ter
Borch. The scene is set in a dark
apothecary's shop, where two ladies
seeking advice are being supplied with
a very special remedy: namely, saus-
ages. Their obscene shape leaves no
doubt as to the erotic ulterior motive
behind the recommended 'treatment.'
The pretended apothecary wears the
costume and mask of Pantaleone, a
comic figure of the Italian Commedia
dell' arte. Active assistance is provided
by a jester in a fool's cap and another
masked man in the background. Act-
ing as the *piskijker*, he examines urine,
urinoscopy being a diagnostic method
that was considered highly questiona-
ble by the 17th century. He thus completes the picture of quackery being
staged here. As the women are not
shown in contemporary dress either,

but wear Renaissance-style clothing,
the whole event perhaps belongs to
the domain of carnival masquerades.
Netscher may also have based his
group on a scene from an unknown
comedy in the theatre.   *HJC*

Gabriel Metsu
1629 Leiden – 1667 Amsterdam

The Cittern Player, about 1662
oak panel, 36.5 x 30 cm – GK 301

The title of this genre painting comes
from a long-forgotten musical instru-

ment. The plucked string instrument that the expensively and colourfully dressed young woman is in the process of tuning in the centre of the picture is not a lute but a cittern. It can be identified by its relatively small, pear-shaped resonant body. The cittern was at the height of its popularity in Metsu's day; in the 18th century it was superseded by the guitar and the mandolin. Music and eroticism are closely related in Renaissance and Baroque art, and the advances of the elegant gentleman holding a half-full glass of wine are to be understood in this sense. Bordering the scene on the right is a still-life painted with detailed attention to the textures. It includes an Oriental rug, commonly used to cover tables in those days, a violin and a drinking-horn. The latter precisely depicts a piece of silversmith's work that was famous in those days and also appears in still-lifes by Willem Kalf: the drinking-horn of the Amsterdam St Sebastian Archers' Guild made in 1565, now on display in the Amsterdam Historical Museum.   *BS*

Jacob Ochtervelt
1634 Rotterdam – 1682 Amsterdam

The Singing Audition, about 1669
canvas, 57.3 x 46 cm – GK 864

Making music together was a leisure-time activity very much appreciated by the Dutch burghers of the 17th century. In genre paintings of the period, singing and playing stringed instruments often also stood metaphorically for the harmony between partners in romantic relationships. This background explains the appearance of the couple in the back of the room in Ochtervelt's painting. They are obviously engaged in amorous conversation. The Latin inscription on the virginals, "MVSYKA MAG[NORUM] SOLAMEN / DVLCE L[ABOR-UM]" (music is sweet solace after heavy work), however, at least as far as the two young ladies in the foreground are concerned, puts the emphasis on the value of music as a pleasant pastime for idle hours. Ochtervelt studied together with Pieter de Hooch under the Haarlem painter Nicolaes Berchem. He concentrated on interiors of this kind mainly between 1660 and 1670.   *HJC*

Gerard ter Borch
1617 Zwolle – 1681 Deventer

Young Woman and Officer Making Music, about 1670
inscr. lower left: G T B (monogram)
canvas, 62 x 47.5 cm – GK 288

As in Ochtervelt's singing scene, the impending or already existing amorous relationship can also be sensed

trary, the discreet expressive gestures of the figures, their elegant clothes with finely painted fabrics, and the furniture and other accessories of evident luxury seem to document a moment in the social life determined by good manners of the Dutch upper middle class. With ambiguous scenes from social life of this kind, ter Borch founded a genre of its own. Many painters tried their hand at it in the second half of the 17th century, including Vermeer.   HJC

between the lines in ter Borch's scene of amateurs making music in a domestic setting. The man and woman are singing a duet, both in the literal (musical) sense and in the metaphorical (erotic) one. The intimate aspect of the situation is emphasised by the setting. This is actually a bedroom, the bed draped with a curtain being visible in the far corner. Yet the painter knows how to keep the scene completely free of vulgarity. On the con-

Philips Wouwerman

1619 Haarlem – 1668 Haarlem

The Piebald at the Forge, about 1658
inscr. lower left: PHILS.W
oak panel, 34.4 x 38.3 cm – GK 362

The usually small-sized pictures by this extremely productive Haarlem genre and landscape painter were extraordinarily popular with aristocratic collectors of the 18th century. Large

collections of them can still be found today in Dresden, St Petersburg, and Kassel. On the one hand Wouwermans was one of the best painters of horses of his day, on the other his approach to figures and landscape is permeated with a charm that appealed to the taste of the age of Rococo. Of the 29 paintings by Philips Wouwerman in the Kassel catalogue of 1783, 20 are still extant. The present work, particularly refined in technique, shows an officer having the horse he uses for riding, an especially high-spirited thoroughbred, re-shod. Beside it is a brown horse, tied up in a wooden contraption, having dental treatment. As required by conditions at the time, the blacksmith's shop is located in the open countryside, far from the village because of the danger of fire.   BS

Frans van Mieris the Younger
1689 Leiden – 1763 Leiden

The Chestnut and Mackerel Vendor, 1722
inscr. upper right: F.V.Mieris Fecit A⁰ 1722
oak panel, 27 x 18.5 cm – GK 312

The motif of the window niche, letting the viewer look from the outside through an arched opening into a domestic or shop room, was an invention introduced into art by Rembrandt's pupil Gerrit Dou around the middle of the 17th century. It became a speciality of the Leiden school. Van Mieris's picture testifies to the continuing popularity of this type of picture even in the 18th century. Its appeal lies in the illusionistic play with pictorial spaces in receding layers. Gestures and objects, such as the vendor's basket, create transitions and even seem to extend into the viewer's space. Moreover, the relief below the windowsill, painted in the same highly precise technique as all the other details, illustrates the theme of the deception of the eye. On the one hand it imitates an actual stone relief by the French sculptor François Duquesnoy, but in painted form. On the other, the children's bacchanal depicted shows a billy goat being fooled by a mask.   HJC

Jan Steen
1626 Leiden – 1679 Leiden

Twelfth Night, 1668
inscr. lower left: JSteen. 1668.
canvas, 82 x 107.5 cm – GK 296

During the 1660s Steen devoted several paintings to the traditional family celebrations of the 'bean feast' on Twelfth Night, the day of Epiphany (see Jordaens, *Twelfth Night* for information on the custom, p. 137). This version shows an especially merry and lively interpretation of the theme. The

prize of being the king for a day has been won by a little boy. Wearing the paper crown, he has been stood on a little table. Only with the help of a grown-up can he comply with the customary obligations to drink. All around, with great hilarity, the others impersonate their roles at court which they have drawn by lot. At the table behind the fool, Jan Steen himself and his wife take part in the game. Meanwhile, the lady in the centre of the scene is already clearly showing the effects of having drunk too much wine.   *HJC*

Adriaen van Ostade
1610 Haarlem – 1685 Haarlem

Merry Country Folk, 1648
inscr. lower right: AV.ostade.1648
canvas, 61 x 51.5 cm – GK 275

Peasant scenes are among the main subjects of Dutch genre painting. Yet they can only be understood when their roots in comedy are taken into consideration. Down to the Age of Enlightenment, the peasant in art and literature is more of a comic figure, stupid and full of all kinds of human vices, than a hard worker and indispensable producer of foodstuffs. However, in the oeuvre of Adriaen van Ostade, the leading Dutch peasant painter, this frequently emphasised negative attitude disappears. The class arrogance of the burgher changes completely into the longing of the oppressed and harried city-dweller for the joys of a carefree country life, as portrayed in idealised form by the Roman poet Horace.

In Ostade's idyllic scene of a country fair, a fiddler and a hurdy-gurdy player are joined by drinking, smoking and amorous peasants. While a pig on the left still recalls the sinful excesses that city people liked to accuse peasants of, an attitude that acknowledges the modest joys of a humble existence with an amused smile has come to the fore.   *BS*

Third Floor

Frederick van Valckenborch
1565/66 Antwerp – 1623 Nuremberg

The Reconciliation of the Romans
and Sabines, about 1605
canvas, 102 x 155 cm – GK 899

The story told by Plutarch and Livy is
one of the myths of the founding of
Rome. As the new city was inhabited
almost only by men, Romulus took
advantage of the opportunity of a celebration, to which the neighbouring
Sabines had been invited, to rape their
women. When the Sabines later conducted a campaign to liberate the ab-
ducted women and invaded the enemy
city, they found out that their wives
and daughters had in the meantime
reconciled themselves to the situation
and feared for their future. Desperate,
they threw themselves between the
warriors and begged for reconciliation. They were successful: from then
on the Romans and the Sabines
formed one nation. Valckenborch's
painting exploits the expressive means
of late Mannerism. The colours are
coolly bright and whitish pale in the
countless schematic figures in the middle ground. In this turbulent scene, the
army of the Romans approaches from
the right and that of the Sabines from
the left, while thoughtfulness and the
will to reconcile arise in the foreground in view of the death of a man.
The picture's theme is thus to be interpreted as a moral exemplar.   *BS*

Pieter Stevens

about 1567 Mechelen (?) –
after 1624 Prague

Mountain Valley with an
Inn and Castle, 1593
oak panel, 45.5 x 67 cm – GK 1063
gift of B. Braun Melsungen AG 1989

In 1594 Pieter Stevens, who had gone
all the way to Rome as a journeyman,
became the first landscape painter at
the court of Emperor Rudolf II in
Prague. His depiction of a swampy
river valley with isolated towering
cliffs, a low mountain landscape possibly inspired by Bohemian and Fran-
conian views, had been painted earlier
and is the first famous painting by this
artist. Originally conceived and extremely finely executed works of this
kind must have helped him obtain this
post. The lack of a view into the distance is innovative and paves the way
for the idyllic close-up landscapes of
the 17th century. Despite a few familiar elements such as the sunlit slope on
the left in the background, the supernatural predominates. On opposite
overgrown banks of the swampy water
are a massive uninhabited ruin of a

castle and an almost derelict inn
(the tiny date of 1593 appears on the
sign), with an approaching couple of
crippled beggars.   BS

Jan Brueghel the Elder

1568 Brussels – 1625 Antwerp

Outpost in a Clearing, 1607
inscr. lower left: BRUEGHEL 1607
oak panel, 32.8 x 42 cm – GK 52

The perspective of a spatially coherent
view, receding continuously into the
depth, is one of the most important in-
novations in landscape painting around
1600. As a specialist in small-scale forest landscapes, Jan Brueghel the Elder
played a decisive part in its development. The *Outpost*, from Landgrave
Wilhelm VIII's collection, illustrates
this perspective clearly. The level
ground of a northern European wood
spreads out before the viewer. A wide
lane along an oblique axis into the distance brings depth into the picture
and provides room for a few figures to
move around in. A group of uncouth
sentry soldiers among them stands out
particularly prominently in the fore-

Collaboration was not unusual among the painters of small cabinet pictures in Antwerp in the early 17th century, and Jan Brueghel the Elder and Hendrick van Balen often worked together. One was specialised in landscapes, flowers and plants, animals and clothed figures, the other mainly in nudes. He had the right to sign the work in this case: "H. van Balen 1608" (lower right). Learned in Venice, his art of softly modelled and gracefully moving nude female bodies is essentially suited to the theme from Greek mythology shown. When the hunter Actaeon was going through the forest, he happened to catch a forbidden glimpse of Artemis (Diana) the goddess of the hunt and her nymphs in the nude while bathing. With a splash of water, the virginal goddess therefore changed him into a deer, which was torn to pieces by his own hounds. While Diana is swinging out her arm to hurl a bowl of water, the fate of Actaeon is already suggested in his daintily sprouting antlers.   *BS*

ground. Their presence reminds us that the forest in the 17th century was not only a place for rustic chores and idyllic walks, but also the dangerous haunt of gangs of thieves and marauding mercenaries that honest people had to protect themselves against.   *HJC*

Hendrick van Balen
about 1575 Antwerp –
1632 Antwerp

and Jan Brueghel the Elder
1568 Brussels – 1625 Antwerp

Diana and Actaeon, 1608
copper, 35.5 x 47 cm – GK 64

Johann Rottenhammer
1564 Munich – 1625 Augsburg

Ecco Homo; Pilate Presents Jesus to
the Public after the Flagellation,
about 1597
copper, 31.5 x 39.4 cm – GK 603

The small copper panel is signed on
the lower left: "159./I Rottnham(er)
F/Venetia." Probably painted in 1597,
the painting with its numerous figures
populating the pictorial stage proves to
be a typically Mannerist work. The influences of Jacopo Tintoretto and Jacopo Palma il Giovane can clearly be de-
tected in the slender elongated figures,
in their twisted poses and movements
and in the colours. By translating these
prototypes into a small scale the painter gives the picture its preciousness.
The traditional Ecce Homo group

(Christ with Pilate and a torturer) is
placed on a podium in the background
by Rottenhammer. The foreground is
taken up by a noisy crowd that is only
partly watching the scene from the
Passion and shouting the decisive
"Crucify him!" to Pilate (John 18 and
19). The others are paying attention to
their daily chores. Rottenhammer
went to Rome in 1590 to study the
art of the Renaissance in Italy. From
1595 to 1605 he worked in Venice,
where this picture was painted. He
was famous all over Europe for small
cabinet-pieces.   *JML*

Joos de Momper
1564 Antwerp – 1635 Antwerp

Alpine Landscape, about 1620
oak panel, 95.5 x 120.5 cm – GK 46

In the 16th century Pieter Bruegel the
Elder made the grandeur of the Alps
into a favourite motif of Dutch landscape painting through his drawings
and etchings showing their cragginess
and vastness. Like other travellers to
Italy, he had crossed the Alps himself.
His follower Joos de Momper satisfied
the continuing demand for Alpine

landscapes throughout his very productive career. A member of the Antwerp painters' guild as early as 1581, he basically conformed to the painting technique of his model until the end of his career, which is why questions of dating are difficult to answer. This painting, allocated to the 1620s, is distinguished by its wealth of motifs and differentiated technique. The foreground, with little figures presumably added by Sebastian Vrancx, breaks off abruptly in an old-fashioned manner. The view recedes into the distance to a town on a riverbank. The mountains rise upwards towards the right, richly layered with rock formations in transparent green and brown hues. *BS*

Frans Francken the Younger

1581 Antwerp – 1642 Antwerp

Apelles and the Cobbler, about 1610–15
inscr. lower right: F.FRANCKEN.INV.
copper, 28.6 x 21.9 cm – GK 78

Classical literature celebrates the Greek Apelles, who was active in the 4th century BC, as the most outstanding painter of all of antiquity. Many anecdotes have grown up around his art. Pliny reports that Apelles, despite his outstanding talent and fame, did not hesitate to accept the criticism of a simple cobbler who criticised the way he had depicted a sandal. But when the same shoemaker, encouraged by the attention, also found fault with the depiction of a leg, Apelles, angry now, replied with the famous saying: "Let not the cobbler go beyond his last!"

Francken shifted the scene from ancient times to his own, thus creating a typical cabinet-piece in theme, style and size for the private picture cabinet of an educated collector. Apelles can be seen on the left in the robes of an aristocrat. The painting presented next to him is the one that the cobbler is just beginning to comment on. It shows Alexander the Great, who, according to ancient tradition, allowed himself to be portrayed by Apelles alone. *HJC*

Sebastian Vrancx

1573 Antwerp – 1647 Antwerp

Soldiers Raiding a Convoy, about 1612
oak panel, 54.5 x 87.5 cm – GK 61

The war of religion and independence that divided the Low Countries between south and north and the houses of Hapsburg and Orange, also left profound traces in art. Sebastian Vrancx was the founder of a new genre of battle painting. He was less interested in the dramatic events of battle with gunpowder smoke blowing everywhere than in the gruesome reality

of the horrors of war, which he recorded with sober exactitude.

In our picture an escorted convoy
of waggons transporting goods is
attacked from an ambush by a group
of riders. The carters and their escort
are being massacred and plundered
down to their bare skin. In the midst
of the brutal carnage, the calm of
an armed rider with a lance and an
officer sounding his trumpet seems
almost cynical. The field of battle,
extending right up to the distant
horizon along a wide road, is framed
by trees with and without foliage.
The latter should be interpreted as
a symbol of death.   *BS*

Peter Paul Rubens
1577 Siegen – 1640 Antwerp

The Triumph of the Victor,
about 1614
oak panel, 160.5 x 263 cm – GK 91

Rubens created this monumental, pa-
thos-filled, Baroque painting for the
banqueting hall of the Militia Company of St George in Antwerp in the
midst of the 80-year civil war. It is a
moral and political allegory in a time-
less neo-antique formal idiom, pointing out to the soldiers of the Hapsburg Catholic south the virtues that
applied in their battle against the re-

bellious Protestant provinces in the north. The armed hero in the centre with a bloody sword, enthroned on the prostrate figure of *Rebellion* (with a torch) and *Discord* (with snakes in her hair), is being crowned with a wreath of oak leaves by the winged goddess Victoria. The bound figure of Barbarism pushes his wild bushy head against his knee. The hero, who is turning up his gaze toward higher authority, is approached from the right by a genius with a bundle of crossbow bolts, a symbol for Unity. Below is an altar with the sacred flame of the fatherland. As the various arms indicate, this is what is to be defended. These symbols are topped by the red and silver Hapsburg flag, the only item directly related to contemporary events in the crowded painting. *BS*

Peter Paul Rubens

1577 Siegen – 1640 Antwerp

Mary with Jesus and St John, Worshipped by Penitent Sinners, about 1619
canvas on oak panel, 258 x 204 cm – GK 119

This altarpiece is a typical work of Catholic Counter-Reformation art in Antwerp. With extravagant gestures, it appeals to the emotions of those who pray and aims to inspire repentance and penitence. Mary, enthroned on high like a princess, is the refuge of the sinners, for whom she intercedes with her son. The penitent sinners are the prodigal son from the parable in the Bible and Mary Magdalen, weeping tears of remorse. They are joined by

King David and St Augustine, the most prominent penitent sinners of the Old Covenant and Christianity, respectively. Finally, on the left, led in by St George with a red flag, are the two founders of monastic orders, St Francis and St Dominic, turning fervently towards the Madonna. The painting may have been made for the church of a mendicant order. Traces of cuts in the canvas, which was mounted on wood early on, indicate wilful damage soon after it was set up around 1620, possibly in the course of the 80-year-long war. The piece was purchased as a work by Anthony van Dyck, who collaborated in the painting as Rubens' best assistant. His hand shows most clearly in the coarsely and thickly applied paint on the figure of the prodigal son.   BS

Anthony van Dyck
1599 Antwerp – 1641 London

Portrait of a Spaniard, about 1630
canvas, 200 x 124 cm – GK 121

The expensively dressed young man in red velvet with gold brocade on his sleeve turns casually and self-confidently towards the viewer. His discreet contrapposto pose with one leg engaged and the other free contributes to this impression. The background is filled with motifs that are traditionally part of portraits of aristocrats and princes: rusticated masonry and a column with green drapery. In fact, the picture was long considered the portrait of an Italian nobleman probably from Genoa, where the artist completed many commissions from aristocrats in 1624–27. This was not questioned until recently, when it was found that the comparatively cool colours indicate a somewhat later date of origin in Antwerp, and the lack of a rapier speaks against this being the portrait of a nobleman. The form of the collar (*golilla*) and the hairdo with side-locks suggest that the sitter was a Spaniard living in the port governed by the Spanish Hapsburgs, who had himself portrayed in this form. He is possibly a merchant.   BS

Abraham Janssens
about 1575 Antwerp – 1632 Antwerp

The Sleeping Diana and Nymphs Spied on by Satyrs, about 1620
canvas, 169 x 235 cm – GK 83

The sight of the almost nude virginal goddess of the hunt, Diana, and her entourage is forbidden to mortals and punishable by death (see van Balen, *Diana and Actaeon* p. 125). Two satyrs, carnal natural creatures and compan-

ions of the wine god Bacchus, have nevertheless managed in taking an illicit peek. The arrow of love shot by the flying Amor makes them feel a surge of lust; one of them even dares to uncover the goddess. But a monkey in the tree above symbolises their unsuccessful foolish pursuit. The kill, consisting of birds, hares and a wild boar hanging from a tree, was added by the specialised animal painter Frans Snyders. Abraham Janssens was the leading painter in Antwerp at the beginning of the 17th century; he later had to take a back seat to Rubens. This painting is influenced by a Rubens composition of the same subject. The sculptural smooth modelling of the figures, however, is an unmistakable feature of Janssens's style.

BS

Jan Cossiers
1600 Antwerp – 1671 Antwerp

The Adoration of the Shepherds, about 1630
canvas, 165.5 x 191 cm – GK 112

Mary shows the shepherds crowding in from the left the Baby Jesus lying in a crib; behind her Joseph is watching

the proceedings. The individually characterised figures and the narrative and realistic details, such as the basket of eggs, are very fresh and lively. Jan Cossiers settled in Antwerp in 1628 after a long stay in France and Italy. In this work, which is one of his best known works and of the highest quality, he combines elements from Caravaggio and Rubens. The composition includes motifs from an altarpiece that Rubens painted for Sint Janskerk in Mechelen. The brilliantly colourful palette is also inspired by Rubens. On the other hand, the comparatively cool freshness, the milky *changeant* effect in Mary's dress, and the pronounced contrast between light and dark are based on inspiration picked up by the artist in the south.   *BS*

Pieter Boel
1622 Antwerp – 1674 Paris

Still-Life with Spoils of War
and Domestic Animals, about 1650
inscr. lower left: P.B.f.
canvas, 175 x 200 cm – GK 162

The combination of different still-life motifs and live animals feels Baroquely sumptuous on the one hand and rather surrealistic in its apparent unconnectedness on the other. However, the composition is not meant realistically but symbolically as an allegory. The live creatures, the turkey, hounds, donkey, sheep, goat and cow, are all domestic animals and symbols of a peacefully productive country life. Among the objects, the military items stand out most: the armour, helmet, trumpet and drum. They define the precious items lying next to them as war booty: a large copper bowl and an Oriental rug thrown over a fur-covered treasure trunk. By showing the animals towering above the spoils of war – the turkey is even enthroned on the drum – the painter demonstrates the triumph of peace over war.

In 1648 the Peace of Westphalia ended the Thirty Years' War and the 80 years of civil war in the Low Countries. This original animal and still-life allegory was made during or shortly after the conclusion of the peace treaty and probably refers to it.   *BS*

Anthony van Dyck

1599 Antwerp – 1641 London

Sebastian Leerse with his Wife and
Son, about 1630–32
canvas, 112 x 164 cm – GK 123

Using a view of a landscape as a background, van Dyck staged the representative portrait of the Antwerp merchant Sebastian Leerse (1584–1664)
and his wife Barbara van den Bo-
gaerde. She was Leerse's second wife.
His son Johann Baptist from his first
marriage is standing on the right. It is
likely that the painting was made in
connection with the event of the second marriage, considering that the
spouses' right hands laid one on top of

the other reflect the symbolic act of
joining right hands (*dextrarum junctio*)
during the wedding mass. Furthermore, the merchant's slightly raised
little finger exposes his wife's wedding ring, which was worn on the
index finger.   HJC

Anthony van Dyck

1599 Antwerp – 1641 London

Frans Snyders and his Wife,
about 1621
canvas, 83 x 110 cm – GK 125

Compared to the Leerse family portrait, this double portrait shows the
sitters less monumentally and more

intimately placed. Van Dyck preferred this manner of representation primarily for his artist colleagues. In fact, the painting does show an artist, namely the animal and still-life specialist Frans Snyders (1579–1657) and his wife Margarethe de Vos. The two separate portraits of the spouses now in New York formed the point of departure for this composition, substantially trimmed at the bottom, which should be seen as a replica combining the two.

The spouses sit close together, the familiar position of their arms expressing their affection for each other. Nevertheless, the portrait does not lack a dignified air. This is created by the elegant poses, the expensive clothing and, last but not least, the backdrop of the curtains.

Corresponding to many contemporary artists' view of themselves, van Dyck presents Snyders and his wife as an artist couple that lays claim to a virtually aristocratic status in society.   HJC

David Teniers the Younger
1610 Antwerp – 1690 Brussels

Peasant Dance by a Tavern,
about 1660–70
inscr. lower left: D.TENIERS.FEC
canvas, 167 x 242.5 cm – GK 148

Peasants' outdoor festivities had been a popular theme for Flemish painters since the 16th century, as evidenced by the famous pictures of country fairs by Pieter Bruegel the Elder. David Teniers, the most successful genre painter in the southern Low Countries in the 17th century, also dealt with the theme repeatedly. The version acquired by Landgrave Wilhelm VIII in 1750 shows kermesse (country fair) celebrations in what is for Teniers an unusually monumental form, complete with broad areas of landscape. The merrymakers in the foreground are ingeniously divided into two groups by a diagonal wooden fence. While those in the front yard of the tavern are still drinking or dancing to the tunes of a bagpipe player, the

others beyond the fenced-in area are already struggling with the ill effects of overindulgence in alcohol. The humorous narrative style allows the viewer to feel a certain sympathy even for the drunks. *HJC*

Jacques d'Arthois
1613 Brussels – 1686 Brussels

Landscape with Shepherds, about 1650–60
canvas, 104.5 x 184 cm – GK 165

Shepherds are driving their flock along a sunken road that leads into a gently hilly landscape. A sudden change of weather shows in the sky above. In the distance, the first showers are already lashing down from the clouds of an upcoming thunderstorm over the fields and villages. The painter used the dramatic weather to plunge different parts of his panorama into variable illumination full of atmosphere. He chose bright hues to accent the sunlit areas and the sky in terms of colour as well. D'Arthois may have been inspired by the region south east of Brussels, though this is not likely to be the depiction of actual topographical features. Rather, the viewer sees an ideal landscape, which, in the way it combines individual tall groups of trees to structure the pictorial space, betrays the influence of Rubens' landscapes. *HJC*

Jacob Jordaens
1593 Antwerp – 1678 Antwerp

The Artist with the Family of his Father-in-Law Adam van Noort, about 1615/16
canvas, 166.3 x 148.2 cm – GK 107

When he was 14 years old, Jordaens was sent to become apprenticed to the painter Adam van Noort. As was common practice, the apprentice lived with the master's family, which obviously soon accepted him into their circle. Over the years, Jordaens fell in love with Catharina, the oldest daughter, whom he married after he completed his apprenticeship. The colourful group portrait that shows the lovers surrounded by the other members of

the van Noort family in front of an arbour with foliage, was probably made on the occasion of their engagement, which was no doubt some time before their marriage on 15 May 1616.

The composition originally contained only the portraits of Jordaens, Catharina and her siblings. The portraits of the parents (-in-law) were added later by the artist, somewhat crowded into the upper left corner. Playing the lute and making wreaths of flowers refer allegorically to the meaning of the couple for marital and familial harmony.   *HJC*

Jacob Jordaens

1593 Antwerp – 1678 Antwerp

The Satyr Visiting the Peasant,
about 1620
canvas, 171 x 193.5 cm – GK 101

Outside the great museums of his native land, it is only in Kassel, where his works fill the central skylighted room, that Jordaens can be studied this well. In comparison to Rubens and van Dyck, the two other great Flemish Baroque masters, his art is aimed mainly at the middle class and has pronounced

popular elements. This picture is a good example. Its theme was such a favourite that Jordaens painted it in many variations. It goes back to a fable by the Greek poet Aesop. A satyr, a wild creature with the legs of a goat, wants to get to know the way of life of human beings and asks a peasant in the fields why he is blowing on his hands. In order to warm them, is the answer. The peasant invites him home for a meal, where he blows onto the soup. This time the explanation is: to cool it. The difference is beyond the satyr's understanding and, full of suspicion, he leaves. The lesson that Jordaens connects to the story is humorous: don't trust anyone who says one thing and means another. The artist stages the scene with large figures filling the entire picture space. They are modelled with strong light and dark contrasts, and seen in a monumentalising view from below. *BS*

Jacob Jordaens
1593 Antwerp – 1678 Antwerp

Twelfth Night, about 1635–55
canvas, 243 x 373 cm – GK 108

Even today one can still come across the custom of celebrating Twelfth Night, or Epiphany, on the 6th of January in the Netherlands. Going back to medieval popular tradition, it makes fun of court ceremonial in a vulgar satirical form that used to provide an opportunity to vent the feelings of oppression due to laws and taxes imposed by the rulers. The large families and their friends would gather for an uninhibited 'court' festivity, during which the person who found the bean that had been baked into a cake got to wear a paper crown. Thus crowned king, he distributed court appointments, such as that of the court jester. His main duty was to set the pace for the heavy drinking. Whenever he raised his glass all the others had to imitate him while shouting "the king

drinks!" Jacob Jordaens, who discovered the scene as a subject for art, painted several large versions of the 'bean feast' which number among his masterpieces. This one is from the beginning of the series. His composition was not laid down at the outset but grew, with several additions that can be identified by the seams in the canvas, to its many-figured large size in the course of 15 to 20 years. Here it is the grandfather, seated on the right, who raises his glass of Rhine wine, freshly filled from the caraffe, and incites the guests to drink to his health.

Much as the artist succeeds in showing us a joy of living that we can sympathise with, it could not have been his aim to defend it. Excessive drinking at fairs and other festivities was feared and combated by the Church and the authorities. The fool on the right raises the clay pipe in his hand to a plaque with a saying that warns against the evil consequences of too much wine. In the foreground a greedy dog knocks over a basket with precious glasses. These hints no longer sufficed for Jordaens later. That explains why he enlarged the picture on the left by adding two couples who illustrate specific effects of alcohol: a helpless drunk embodies the vice of sloth and a dashing lover the vice of lechery. Nevertheless, as always with Jordaens, even these warnings are made not with a wagging finger but a sense of humour. <small>BS</small>

Jacob Jordaens
1593 Antwerp – 1678 Antwerp

The Childhood of Jupiter,
about 1640–50
canvas, 219 x 247 cm – GK 103

Ever since the Renaissance, the childhood of Jupiter, the father of the gods, provided painting with some of its

most favourite themes from Greek mythology. The account by the Classical poet Hesiod reports the events involved: In order to circumvent the prophecy that he would be ousted from his throne by a son, the Titan Saturn devoured each of his children right after birth. However, his wife delivered the youngest, Jupiter, secretly in Crete and had him hidden and raised on goat's milk by the nymph Adrasteia. This upbringing of the hidden boy forms the subject of Jordaens's painting. The toddler Jupiter, Adrasteia next to the goat, a satyr and another nymph are shown in ideal nudity, suitably enough for the arcadian subject-matter, providing the artist plenty of opportunity to demonstrate his ability at depicting human bodies.

In addition, the boy's obvious crying over the spilt milk shown in connection with the satyr's flute playing brings another textual source into play. For according to Ovid, baby Jupiter's cries had to be drowned out with music on Crete in order to prevent his discovery by Saturn.   *HJC*

David Teniers the Younger
1610 Antwerp – 1690 Brussels

Peasants Playing Cards, 1633
oak panel, 31.5 x 53.5 cm – GK 139

Peasant interiors contributed substantially to Teniers's success as a genre painter. This painting is one of his earliest dated works and, as usual with interiors of inns by the Flemish painter, takes its basic pictorial elements from an unchanging repertoire of motifs that are varied in only a few details. These include the card players, the beret hanging in the door, and the man warming himself in front of the fireplace in the back room. The very uncouth, boorish character of the figures still betrays the influence of Brouwer, whose satirically portrayed peasants Teniers transformed into more likeable characters. A special feature is the cellar door on the far right, adding a third space to what are usually two in Teniers's paintings. Around it the painter has arranged pieces of firewood, a broom and other household supplies into a rustic still-life. The drawing hung over the mantelpiece, a typical form of wall decoration at the time, bears the date.   *HJC*

Peter Paul Rubens

1577 Siegen – 1640 Antwerp

The Flight into Egypt, 1614
inscr. lower right: P.P.RVBENS. F.1.6.1.4
oak panel, 40.5 x 53 cm

This delicately painted cabinet-piece is one of the few works by this painter that he has provided with his signature. It was painted as an homage to Adam Elsheimer, his late friend and the outstanding master of small formats whom he had met in Rome. However, unlike the latter's *Flight into Egypt* (Munich, Alte Pinakothek), where the landscape predominates, Rubens's piece focuses on the monumentally conceived group of figures. Angels guide the Holy Family; with their protection Mary rides the donkey in an unafraid upright position. A supernatural light emanates from the Christ Child, making the blue and red colour accents of Mary's clothing light up. The drama of the escape is expressed by the way Joseph turns around to where one of King Herod's horsemen can be seen in pursuit on the shore in the distance. The moon reflected in the water is a direct quote from Elsheimer's painting and a reference to that artist's inventive landscapes.

BS

Frans Snyders

1579 Antwerp – 1657 Antwerp

Still-Life with Game, Birds, Grapes and Vegetables, about 1613
inscr. lower right: F. snyders. fecit.
oak panel, 57 x 89 cm – GK 116a

Among the Flemish still-life painters of the 17th century, Snyders is the

most prodigious. No one else produced flower, fruit and animal pictures as brilliantly and copiously as he did. Many of them were realised in collaboration with Rubens, whose figure scenes were expanded by Snyders by means of still-life arrangements as opulent as they were intricate. The present work does without a staffage of figures, concentrating instead on the colourful presentation of the superimposed bodies of animals from the kill in addition to fruit, vegetables and various items of tableware, including a Chinese porcelain plate. The painter's skilful brushstroke makes the various different textures of the surfaces appear realistic. The complicated intermingling of animals and fruits follows the organisational pattern of a new variation on the still-life that he established himself. The preparatory drawing for this painting is preserved in the Louvre in Paris.   *HJC*

Jacques de l'Ange
active about 1631 – 1642 in Antwerp

Avarice: Old Woman Weighing Gold, 1642
canvas, 126 x 103.5 cm – GK 183

Avarice is one of the seven deadly sins against which the good Christian must defend himself. Especially in old age, when physical attractiveness has faded, the danger of succumbing to miserliness increases. This traditional idea forms the basis for this scene of an old woman weighing gold in an office. As a representation of avarice, it was originally part of a cycle of seven paintings, one for each deadly sin. The little-known Antwerp painter Jacques de l'Ange was identified as the artist only

recently. In order to underscore the symbolic significance of his picture, he had the old woman joined by a young horned devil and a greedy swindler. While the one tries to encourage temptation with more gold, the other is already enviously eyeing the woman's property that he would love to relieve her of quickly. This painting comes alive through the light of the oil lamp. Its date can be found inscribed on the bags of money in the background.   *HJC*

Cornelis van Poelenburch
1594/95 Utrecht – 1667 Utrecht

The Martyrdom of St Lawrence, 1620/21
copper, 35.4 x 44 cm – GK 209

From the end of the 16th century on, the voyage to Italy increasingly became part of the self-imposed training programme of Dutch painters. Van Poelenburch belongs to the first generation of painters who also translated their impressions directly into Italianate pictures. This attempt is demonstrated by *The Martyrdom of St Lawrence*, which

was painted while he was still in Italy, where he stayed for several years. Thus an urban architecture that clearly refers to the ruins of Roman antiquity forms the background for the martyrdom, which according to the legend took place in the Holy City in 258. At that time the deacon Laurentius was roasted alive on an iron grill after he had distributed the property of the Church among the poor instead of delivering it to Emperor Valerian and abjuring the Christian faith.   HJC

Bartholomeus Breenbergh

1598 Deventer – 1657 Amsterdam

Landscape with Ruins and
Saints Peter and John, about 1625
inscr. lower right: BB.f.
copper, 24 x 33.3 cm – GK 205

Like van Poelenburch, Breenbergh, who had spent a decade in Rome himself, painted works influenced strongly by the example of Italy starting in the 1620s. In this painting with

the two apostles, the towering ruin with fragments of ancient brick vaults, the rocky infertile fields and, last but not least, the warm yellowish flood of sunlight create the impression of a Mediterranean scene. The actual Biblical event only takes up the lower right corner. Several members of the first community of Christians, who gave their possessions to St Peter and St John to distribute among the needy (according to the story of the apostles in Acts 4, 32–37), can be identified. Breenbergh's hand differs from van Poelenburch's especially in the more spontaneous, less enamel-like technique in the human figures.   *HJC*

Frans Hals

1582/83 Antwerp – 1666 Haarlem

Portrait of a Man; Portrait of a Woman, about 1618–20
canvas on wood, 102.5 x 79 cm;
103 x 82.5 cm – GK 213; GK 214

Dutch portraiture found its best and, with increasing production, also most creative representative in Frans Hals. The two portraits that Landgrave Wilhelm VIII bought in 1752 belong to the early work of the artist. They are still strongly dependent on the older, more severe Netherlandish scheme for portraits of married couples. Both spouses stand facing each other symmetrically, whereby the man, according to the heraldic tradition, is on the right (= left seen by the viewer), the position of honour that is his due. The light shines consistently from the left in both pictures. This makes the woman's face more brightly and evenly lit across the whole surface, which was commonly thought advantageous to her womanly charms. The shadows in the backgrounds stand

out as an unusual device intended to loosen up the stiffness of the poses. Despite the coats of arms that have been included, it has not been possible to identify the sitters.   *HJC*

Frans Hals
1582/83 Antwerp – 1666 Haarlem

Peeckelhaering (The Merry Drinker), about 1640–43
canvas, 75 x 61.5 cm – GK 216

In Dutch folk comedy the 'Pickled Herring' character plays a role corresponding to that of the village idiot or a buffoon. The black-haired man is made up to look dark-skinned, wears red clothes trimmed with yellow bands and a red and yellow cap, and gives the viewer a glazed look. In his hand is the typical (wine) jug, from which he quenches his chronic thirst. Above the jug appears the signature "f.hals f." Hals may have portrayed a famous actor playing his role. Red and

yellow had characterised the fool's costume since the 16th century. "The wet jug must tempt him / for his throat is always dry" reads the inscription under a contemporary print that reproduces the painting. Jan Steen (1626–1679) cites the popular picture in two of his paintings. Hals's high-spirited touch, broad brushstrokes and bold light and dark effects convey a merry, spontaneous impression rarely achieved in 17th-century portraiture.   *JML*

Frans Hals
1582/83 Antwerp – 1666 Haarlem

Man in a Slouch Hat, about 1660
canvas, 79.5 x 66.5 cm – GK 219

The Kassel Gallery's major painting by Frans Hals, signed "F H" above the man's left shoulder, is one of his late works. With a pronouncedly casual air, the sitter turns sideways on his chair and lets his arm hang over the back. The unidentified man turns his head, which is covered with a large, black, slouch hat, to face the viewer directly.

He seems to be telling us something or is about to say something witty. The composition is determined by intersecting diagonals. The colour black clearly predominates over red, white, yellow and grey. In the subtle overall impression of colour thus created, the serious black stands for the honourable, self-confident burgher of good class. Nevertheless, his pose and his jovial expression indicate that he is in the prime of life and seeking to make contact with the viewer.

A copy of this 'proto-Impressionist' masterpiece was made by Lovis Corinth (1907) and is in the Neue Galerie in Kassel.   *JML*

Pieter de Grebber

about 1600 Haarlem – 1653 Haarlem

Belshazzar's Feast, 1625
inscr. bottom centre: P DG AN 1625
oak panel, 151 x 223 cm – GK 221

Belshazzar, the last King of Babylon, had the golden vessels stolen by his father Nebuchadnezzar from the Temple of Jerusalem brought to be used at a great feast. A mysterious hand appeared and wrote signs on the wall that only the wise Jew Daniel was able to interpret. They announced the end of the king's power and the division of his kingdom. Belshazzar was assassinated that very night.

Although Pieter de Grebber had visited Rubens in Antwerp in his youth, he tells the dramatic story without Baroque agitation and bright colours but with remarkably light hues. Petrifying fear has seized the king and his court. Everyone is staring with wide-open eyes at the hand of God coming out of a cloud and writing the ominous enigmatic signs. The inner tension is also expressed by the strongly contrasting light and shadow falling on the figures. The provenance of the large picture, a key work of early Dutch Neo-Classicism, is the formerly Danish castle of Gottorf near Schleswig. It may have been painted for the Copenhagen court, which was partial to monumental painting in this style.   BS

Melchior de Hondecoeter
1636 Utrecht – 1695 Utrecht

The White Peacock, about 1670/90
inscr. on the pedestal in the centre: M. D. Hondecoeter
canvas, 144 x 180.5 cm – GK 381

A specialist in painting live fowl, Hondecoeter usually featured domestic and exotic species of birds in ever new combinations in decorative paintings that were very much in demand in his lifetime. Here an imaginary palace park serves as a backdrop for a procession of birds joined by a little monkey,

a guenon (*Cercopithecus* species) to be precise, on the balustrade. The scene is dominated by a white peacock in a threatening pose, trying to chase away a pheasant. The artist uses their conduct to introduce a narrative element that loosens up the side-by-side presentation of the birds. Concealed in the birds' behaviour is also a play on traditional allegorical meanings. Similar to the peacock, the pheasant had also been a symbol of worldly splendour, coupled with vanity and pride, ever since antiquity. Rivalling the peacock as a symbol in paintings, it often took the latter's place.   HJC

Rembrandt Harmensz. van Rijn
1606 Leiden – 1669 Amsterdam

Half-Figure of an Old Man with a Gold Chain, 1632
inscr. right centre: RHL van Ryn 1632
oak panel, 59.3 x 49.3 cm – GK 233

Pictures of individuals attain a height of their development in Rembrandt's oeuvre, whether in portraits of famous

Rembrandt Harmensz. van Rijn

1606 Leiden – 1669 Amsterdam

Portrait of a Man Sharpening a Quill,
1632
inscr. right, on the paper: RHL
(in monogram) van Rÿn 1632
canvas, 104.5 x 84.5 cm – GK 234

Because of his outstanding ability in
portraiture, Rembrandt soon became
very much in demand after he settled
in Amsterdam in 1631. Among the first
works he was commissioned there was
this portrait of a man sharpening a
quill, in which the master already applied his entire range of artistic invention. By doing without any obvious
pose, the sitter is encountered in a very
private atmosphere that feels familiar
and realistic. The man seems to have
interrupted his writing for only a short
time to trim his quill, whereby his gaze
seems directed naturally towards the
viewer. The positioning of the hands
almost exactly in the centre of the picture gives the everyday activity a larger
meaning. Writing with well-main-
tained equipment is evidently charac-

and high-ranking personalities, or of
Biblical or historical figures, or in
character studies of interesting types,
of which this painting is an example.
The genre was called *tronie*, which
means a face enlivened by mime.
Rembrandt liked to focus on old people with wrinkled faces marked by life.
He used professional models who also
reappear in paintings by the Rembrandt school but are not known by
name. The powerful striking type of
old man in our picture, with his broad
face, meaty nose and bushy eyebrows,
inspired Rembrandt to use an expressive technique with thickly applied
paints that would be unthinkable for
commissioned portraits (see *Man
Sharpening a Quill*, 1632). This 'study of
a head' acquired additional importance
as a prototype for contemporary
history and genre painting.   *BS*

teristic of the sitter. This suggests that he is a teacher, writer or calligrapher. Moreover, trimming a quill can be understood as a common symbol for diligent practice. This was considered one of the virtues and pillars of success of all reputable artists and scholars.

The portrait, worked out in virtuoso fashion, has a companion-piece in the Vienna Academy collection showing a similarly unidentified woman. It was painted on a piece of canvas cut from the same bolt of fabric as the painting in Kassel. *HJC*

Rembrandt Harmensz. van Rijn
1606 Leiden – 1669 Amsterdam

Saskia van Uylenburgh in Profile,
about 1634–1642
oak panel, 99.5 x 78.8 cm – GK 236

In the few years between 1633 and 1642, between their engagement and her death, Rembrandt's wife Saskia van Uylenburgh plays a prominent role in his art both as a model and in portraits. This painting, outstanding among his works, kept the artist occupied for years. It was begun soon after their engagement. Rembrandt often used the profile motif at that time, as in his portrait of the wife of the reigning

Stadholder at the court of The Hague. Here it contributes to the festive and remote impression of the pale, delicately modelled face against a dark background. His signature with the date of 1642 is documented but no longer visible.

The artist evidently did not complete the picture until after Saskia's death, doing so in her memory. The swaying feather on her hat is a sign of the transience of life, the sprig (of rosemary?) in her hand a symbol of steadfast fidelity. Only at this point was the utterly sumptuous and minutely painted ornament of pearls, gold and brocade laboriously added. The Renaissance costume, worn for patrician roles on the stage in those days, removes Saskia completely from everyday life. It was understood as a reference to classical antiquity. *BS*

Rembrandt Harmensz. van Rijn
1606 Leiden – 1669 Amsterdam

Jacob Blessing Ephraim and Manasseh, 1656
inscr. lower left: Rembran / f. 1656
canvas, 173 x 209 cm – GK 249

Besides portraiture, Rembrandt also excelled in the sensitive narrative portrayal of Bible stories. The painting of *Jacob Blessing the Sons of Joseph* is the result of his interpretation of an account in Genesis 48. Just before the very old patriarch Jacob died, he blessed his grandsons Manasseh and Ephraim by laying on his hands, thus placing them on an equal footing with his own sons through this act of adoption. Defying tradition, the blessing of the younger Ephraim occurred with Jacob's right hand, while the older brother Manasseh merely received a blessing from the

less significant left hand. When Joseph, the boys' father, tried to correct the apparent mistake made by his own, almost blind, father Jacob in favour of the first-born, the patriarch countered: "I know, my son, I know, ..., this also shall become peoples ... but this younger brother shall be greater than he: and his seed shall grow into nations."

In Rembrandt's reading, the important event that incorporated Jacob's grandsons into the circle of Israel's founding fathers and, moreover, gave Ephraim a superior position, becomes an intimate family scene. The solemnity of the moment when the aged Jacob blesses the little Ephraim from his bed is excellently expressed. Joseph only seems to be supporting the right hand that gives the blessing; his attempt to pull it over to the older brother is no longer evident. By deviating slightly from the biblical text, Rembrandt heightened the impression made by his depiction even more. Thus the boys are not standing separately on either side of the bed, but together and close to their parents on the grandfather's left. Ephraim, moreover, crosses his arms in front of his chest. This, together with the pale nimbus round his head, refers symbolically his future interpretation as the Old Testament precursor of the Christians.

Their mother Asenath, whose face and stance indicate her affectionate feelings and emphasise the seriousness of the event, does not appear at all in the relevant Biblical passage. With mostly pastose, free brushstrokes, Rembrandt succeeded most convincingly in developing not only the essential gestures and emotions of his figures but also the different textures of the Oriental robes. Equally convincingly, he captured the physical features and the typical behaviours of three ages of man: childhood, maturity and old age. The surreal, bright highlighting emphasises the individual figures while joining them into a self-contained group at the same time. Various traces of reworking indicate that the artist worked for a considerable time on completing this famous painting. *HJC*

Govert Flinck

1615 Cleves – 1660 Amsterdam

Portrait of Margaretha Tulp as a Bride, 1655
inscr. upper right: G.Flinck f. 1655
canvas, 138 x 103.5 cm – GK 1062

Like Rembrandt, from whom he gained a lot of experience as an apprentice, Flinck became a portraitist much in demand by the Amsterdam middle class. Contributing to his lasting success was his continual adapta-

tion to the latest fashions. As early as the mid-1640s, Flinck stopped following Rembrandt in favour of a new style oriented on van Dyck's portraits. Its fully developed features are illustrated in his portrait of Margaretha Tulp. The young lady is presented in an expensive silk dress and extremely elegant pose in front of a garden view enhanced by representative architectural elements.

The picture, dating from the year the daughter of the famous doctor Nicolaes Tulp married the influential mayor Jan Six, is filled with symbolism. Most symbolic is the bouquet of flowers being freshened in a fountain topped by Amor, symbolising the blossoming as well as the endurance of the bride's love. The pearls at her ears, around her neck and on her dress refer to her first name (pearl = *margarita* in Latin) while the tulip on the balustrade stands for her family name.   HJC

Gerbrand van den Eeckhout
1621 Amsterdam – 1674 Amsterdam

Christ and the Woman Taken in Adultery, 1653
inscr. lower left: G V Eeckhout 1653
canvas, 61 x 79.5 cm – GK 1064

According to the Gospel of St John (8: 2–11) the Jewish Pharisees and scribes confronted Jesus in front of the Temple of Jerusalem with a woman who was caught in the act of committing adultery. In order to put the Saviour to the test, they asked his opinion on the prescribed punishment of stoning. Christ answered with the famous words: "He that is without sin among you, let him first cast a stone at her." This is exactly the moment that Eeckhout chose for his painting. The modelling of the figures in Oriental robes, their arrangement in front of the dark, diffuse background of the temple, and particularly the overall warm hues of the palette

define it unmistakably as the work of a Rembrandt pupil. The picture follows Rembrandt's more monumental interpretation of the same subject, preserved in London in the National Gallery. As an apprentice and later also as a friend, Eeckhout was held in especially high esteem by Rembrandt and followed the example of his teacher in his history pictures all his life.   *HJC*

Pieter Lastman

1583 Amsterdam – 1633 Amsterdam

Abraham Hosting the Three Angels, 1616
inscr. lower left: Pietro Lastman fecit Anno MVIXVI
canvas, 82 x 126 cm – L 1145

At the beginning of the 17th century, Lastman came into contact with the paintings of Caravaggio, the Carraccis and Adam Elsheimer in Italy. Their formal inventions, such as strong contrasts between dark and light and between different colours, came to be incorporated into his oeuvre. It consists largely of pictures of Biblical stories, such as this one based on a story in Genesis. God had three angels announce to the patriarch Abraham in the grove of Mamre that his wife Sarah, despite her old age, would still conceive a son (Genesis 18: 1–15).

Lastman seated the winged guests on a carpet that also forms the base for a still-life documenting the generosity of the host. The use of a carpet as a surface to dine on and the clothing worn by Abraham bring an Oriental touch to the picture otherwise inspired by Netherlandish landscapes. Lastman himself made two other versions of this popular theme, of which one is considered lost while the other shows the arrival of the angels at Abraham's house (St Petersburg, Hermitage). Around 1619–25 Lastman passed his artistic expertise on to his apprentices, Jan Lievens and Rembrandt.   *HJC*

Moses van Uyttenbroeck

1595/1600 The Hague –
1646/47 The Hague

The Judgement of Paris, 1626
inscr. bottom centre: 1626 / Mᴼ. v. WBK
(in monogram)
oak panel, 37.5 x 39 cm – GK 190

Zeus, the father of the gods, resolved
that Paris was to be the cause of the
Trojan War. The point of departure for
the whole event was when the Trojan
prince was called to play the role of
a judge in the question of whether
Hera, Athena or Aphrodite should re-
ceive the prize for the being the most
beautiful. Each of the three goddesses
offered a reward for being chosen. In
the end, Paris decided to choose Aphrodite, who had promised him marriage to Helen. Her subsequent ab-
duction was what started the war
with the Greeks. Uyttenbroeck's
painting shows the moment just after
the decision, for the naked Aphrodite
is already holding the apple that is the
sign of her triumph. Posing on either
side of her are her divine competitors.
According to Apuleius's account (*The*

Golden Ass, X), their clothing suggests
the reward they promised: glory in
war (armed Athena) or glory in king-
ship (crowned Hera). Paris himself is
shown as a shepherd, which is how
legend has him growing up. The
beauty contest was moved to an Italianate landscape. Uyttenbroeck was
appointed by the ruling family of the
northern Netherlands in 1638 as a
specialist in history painting.   *HJC*

Jacob Pynas

about 1592 Amsterdam – after 1652,
place unknown

Landscape with the Meeting of Moses
and Aaron, about 1620
copper, 21 x 27.2 cm – GK 612

This painter was one of Adam
Elsheimer's followers and preferred to
work in a small-scale detailed technique on copper. Along with Rembrandt's teacher Pieter Lastman, he
is classed with a group of artists that
art historical research has called the
'Pre-Rembrandtists' because of the
many Biblical themes predominating

in their work. The Old Testament episode in this picture has rarely been depicted in art. The two brothers, Moses and Aaron, had orders from Yahweh to lead the Israelites out of Egypt together. Moses, who had already fled the country long ago, was ordered to return, and Aaron to advance towards him in the desert. They met by the mountain of God, Horeb, and embraced. Pynas lends emphasis to this moment by having Aaron run the last bit towards his brother and by setting the pair off from his entourage. Painted in jewel-like colours, the picture is dominated by a mountain landscape full of atmosphere in high-contrast, warm light.

BS

Adriaen van de Venne

1589 Delft – 1662 The Hague

Banquet in a Park Landscape near a Palace, 1617
inscr. bottom centre: AV. VENNE 1617
copper, 12.6 x 17.8 cm – GK 211

The tiny painting shows a summer party with many figures near a Renaissance palace. Sitting around a big table set with a white tablecloth, men

and women are enjoying familiar conversation at a sumptuous meal. One couple is stepping out for the dance to the music of lutes and violas. A horseman and a fisherman can be seen at the edge of the forest; beyond it people are merrily playing ball on a large meadow. This kind of scene of people enjoying life was popular in Holland in the early 17th century, when the economic boom suddenly caused prosperity to spread. Art also warned against the excesses of the life of the new rich. Van de Venne, a master of satire in many of his pictures, includes a discreet piece of moral advice in this one: in front of the gate in the hedge around the palace garden, the prodigal son of the Biblical parable, who had squandered his money among whores, is being chased out into the street. BS

Hendrick ter Brugghen

1588 Utrecht – 1629 Utrecht

Boy Playing a Flute, 1621
inscr. on the hat: HTB

Boy Playing a Recorder, 1621
inscr. centre left: HTBrugghen.fecit.1621
canvas, 71.3 x 55.8 cm each – GK 179;
GK 180

After completing his training, ter Brugghen lived in Rome for several years. There he was decisively influenced by the revolutionary realism of Caravaggio, which he mixed with elements of northern style. In Utrecht he became the leading master of a group of Caravaggists that set the tone in the northern Low Countries after 1620. These two flute players of 1621 are prime examples of pictures of life-sized half-figures of individual musicians, drinkers and other folksy figures that were much sought after. They are conceived as contrasting companion-pieces in both form and content. The transverse flute player in the striped lansquenet's outfit stands for the military and urban world; the recorder player in the shepherd's costume for the rustic, arcadian one. Ever since classical literature (Horace), country life had been idealised from the point of view of the city-dweller.

This is also reflected in ter Brugghen's work. In pronounced contrasts, cool colours dominate in the transverse flute player's portrait, warm ones in the recorder player's; the face of the one is in shadow against a ruined, disintegrating wall in the background, that of the other lit up against an intact surface. *BS*

Jan Lievens
1607 Leiden – 1674 Amsterdam

Fire and the Age of Childhood, about 1623–25
oak panel, 83 x 58.2 cm – GK 1205

The pastose dynamic application of paint distinguishes Lievens's early work. This indicates that he painted his cycle of the four elements and ages of man (GK 1205–1208) after the completion of his apprenticeship with Pieter Lastman in 1621 and before the beginning of his fruitful collaboration with the young Rembrandt after 1625. The first picture in the cycle is devoted to the element of fire, which is combined with the age of childhood. It shows a boy trying to light a torch with a red-hot piece of coal. In order to fan the fire he blows hard, puffing out his cheeks, onto the coal. Its flickering up is the only source of light for the scene. With complicated illumination of this kind, Lievens was not only taking on a demanding artistic task but also seeking to follow and compete with ancient art. For according to literary sources, the best painters of the ancient world had already considered the depiction of a scene with nothing but an artificial source of light an extraordinary artistic challenge. *HJC*

Rembrandt Harmensz. van Rijn

1606 Leiden – 1669 Amsterdam

Winter Landscape, 1646
inscr. lower left: Rembrandt f. 1646
oak panel, 16.6 x 23.4 cm – GK 241

Views of landscapes not only play a
role in the backgrounds of history
scenes in Rembrandt's work. They
also appear in a few of his paintings
between 1630 and 1650 that do completely without a mythological or
Biblical framework. The aim of these
independent landscapes is to evoke
certain lighting conditions as well as
atmospheric and climatic ambience.
By purchasing the *Winter Landscape*
dated 1646, Landgrave Wilhelm VIII
acquired an impressive and, moreover,
especially rare example of a Rembrandt landscape. It is particularly rare
because it is the only known painting
of winter by the artist. Moreover,
there was nothing comparable in existence in painting at the time. The
rapid, sketchy application of the paint
depicts a few buildings and inhabi-
tants of a village around a frozen lake.
The blue light makes the frosty cold
of the air almost palpable. The peasant
figures seem, nevertheless, to be enjoying the meagre sunshine of a typical winter day with calm satisfaction
as they go about their daily chores.
The immediacy of the scene is remarkable. It seems to have been encountered by the artist, unlike, for in-
stance, the view in Rembrandt's *River
Landscape with a Windmill* (GK 242),
which can immediately be recognised
as a pastiche purely from the artist's
imagination.   *HJC*

Rembrandt Harmensz. van Rijn

1606 Leiden – 1669 Amsterdam

The Holy Family with a Curtain, 1646
inscr. on the railing: Rembrandt ft. 1646
oak panel, 46.8 x 68.4 cm – GK 240

In the 1640s Rembrandt was partial
to intimate domestic scenes and he
created several pictures of the Holy
Family, of which this painting is the
most original and independent. The
wooden panel, trimmed at the upper
corners, shows a painting on the subject of the Holy Family as well as an
elaborately ornamented gold frame
with a rod and a curtain attached to
it. In the many-layered pictorial concept, the curtain serves the function

of both a piece of equipment that was actually used for paintings and a device that interprets the religious image. It exposes the left half with Mary and the Christ Child but covers parts of the right with Joseph, who can be seen doing carpentry in the background. Joseph, standing outside the house, represents the Old Covenant, which, according to St Paul, becomes shrouded in darkness with the birth of Christ and the beginning of the New Law. Mary hugs the child closely and gazes with pensive foreboding into the fire. The latter, with the bowl of porridge and a purring cat, forms a harmless, cosy still-life in the centre that distracts us from the profoundly intellectual play of ideas.   BS

Esaias van de Velde
1587 Amsterdam – 1630 The Hague

Winter Landscape, about 1629
inscr. bottom centre: E.V.VELDE.1629.
oak panel, 36.7 x 58.1 cm – GK 384

Wintry scenes of villages and fields constitute a frequently recurring theme in Esaias van de Velde's oeuvre. They provide the artist, who is one of the fathers of landscape painting in the northern Low Countries, numerous opportunities for experimentation with narrative, compositional and colour effects. In this village landscape, which dates from van de Velde's late period, the accent is on cleverly wrought interrelationships between

varying intensities of light and colour, combined in an overall winter atmosphere and, almost incidentally, giving the scenery spatial depth. Mighty trees rise up in the foreground, their bare dark trunks and branches seem even darker against the snow-covered rooftops emanating light in the middle ground. By contrast, the distance and the sky step back in less contrasting hues and form a subtly gradated, wintry subdued, foil in the background. Several skaters can be distinguished in the lower left quarter of the picture.   HJC

Karel van Mander III

1606 Delft – 1670 Copenhagen

Hydaspes and Persina in Front of Andromeda's Picture, about 1640
canvas, 110 x 220 cm – GK 1167

This is the first of a cycle of nine wide, frieze-like paintings of scenes from the romance, *Aethiopica*, by the late antique writer Heliodorus. The artist painted

them around 1640 for the castles of the Danish King Christian IV, whence they came via Sweden to Kassel before 1749. The love story was popular in Holland mainly during the early 17th century and also served as a source for other painters. Karel van Mander knew best how to translate the dramatic turns of the plot into a lively pictorial idiom.

The picture shows the dark-skinned Ethiopian royal couple, Hydaspes and Persina. During their love-making the queen looked intensely at the picture of Andromeda, the mythical Greek progenitor of the royal family, and thereupon gave birth to a white-skinned daughter. Chariclea was rejected and ended up in Greece, where Theagenes was inflamed with love or her. After perilous adventures, trials and separations, the two were happily reunited in Ethiopia.   BS

The Collection
of Prints and Drawings

The History of the Collection of Prints and Drawings

Christiane Lukatis

The entire collection comprises about 45,000 prints and drawings. They are arranged chronologically into drawings and printed works, subdivided by country, artist and subject, i.e. into portraiture and topography. An alphabetical card catalogue indexes the most of the graphic art.

Up to the 19th century, it was customary to preserve graphic art by pasting prints into bound portfolios. While these albums were disassembled long ago in other print rooms, 45 precious 18th-century leather-bound volumes with prints have been preserved in Kassel. These volumes of pasted prints were formerly part of the collections of the landgraves of Hesse-Kassel. They contain mainly prints after famous paintings and works of ancient art. The amply filled volume of engravings and woodcuts by Albrecht Dürer was taken apart in 1916, so that these prints are now

*Ludwig Emil
Grimm,
Bettina von
Arnim, 1809*

Oeuvres de Phil. Wouwermans gravées par J. Moyreau

1. Retour de la Chasse et Curée	36. L'Hyver
2. Départ pour la Chasse au Vol	37. Les Maquignons a la foire
3. La Chasse aux Canards	38. Petite Chasse a l'oiseau
4. La Marchande de marée	39. Pillage des Reitres pendant les guerres Civiles sous Henri IV en 1587
5. Grande Chasse a l'oiseau	40. La Famille du Maréchal
6. L'Abbreuvoir	41. L'Abbreuvoir des Chasseurs
7. Le Passage de l'eau	42. Le Marchand de foin
8. Course de la Prague	43. L'Académie du Manege
9. Les Marchands de Chevaux	44. Le Défilé d'Equipages
10. La Buvette des Chasseurs	45. Gardes de Cavallerie
11. Le Cabaret	46. Le Marchand de Mitridate
12. La Fontaine des Chasseurs	47. Le petit pont de bois
13. La Petite Chasse au Cerf	48. L'Embrasement du moulin
14. La Cascade	49. La Défaite des Sarasins
15. L'Ecurie	50. Les Chasseurs Sortans de la Forêt
16. Fêtes et Adieux des Chasseurs	51. Le Bouffon des Chasseurs
17. L'Arrivée des Chasseurs	52. Les Bohémiens
18. Le Grand Marché aux Chevaux	53. Le Travail du Maréchal
19. Quartier Général de l'Armée hollandaise	54. La Chaumiere
20. Grande Chasse au Cerf	55. La Diligence Hollandoise
21. La Boutique du Maréchal	56. L'Accident du Chasseur
22. La Fontaine de Bachus	57. La Fontaine de Neptune
23. Départ pour la Chasse aux Chiens couchant	58. Le Port au Foin
24. Guerre des Huguenots sous Charles IX en 1562	59. La Grotte du Maréchal
25. Oeuvres de Phil. Wouwermans ...	60. Les Marchands forains
26. Le Colombier du Maréchal	61. La Baraque du Pêcheur
27. Les Baigneurs	62. L'Abbreuvoir Hollandois
28. Quartier de Rafraichissement	63. La Buvette des Dames
29. Prédication de St Jean Baptiste	64. La Fontaine du Triton
30. La Chasse aux Eperviers	65. La Fontaine de Vénus
31. Le Présent du Chasseur	66. La Charité des Capucins
32. La Conduite des Dames pour la Chasse	67. Le Conseil des Chasseurs
33. La petite Foire aux Chevaux	68. Recreation militaire
34. L'Ecurie Hollandoise	69. Marche d'Armée
35. Le Vin de l'Etrillé	70. Cavaliers du Manege

Landgrave Wilhelm IX.
Table of contents of the album of "Oeuvres de Phil. Wouwermans gravées par F. Moyreau,"
after 1785

available individually. Old master drawings comprise a small collection emphasising the art of the Netherlands and of Italy in the 16th and 17th centuries. They include works by Paul Bril, Abraham Bloemaert, Jan van Goyen, and Paolo Veronese. Single but especially high-quality drawings by Albrecht Dürer (see p. 165, 166, 168), Johann Liss and Mattias Gundelach round off this section. 18th- and 19th-century artists of the Kassel Academy of Art, such as the members of the Tischbein, Ruhl, and Nahl families of artists, Wilhelm Böttner, Johann Erdmann Hummel and

71.	Occupations Champêtres	102.	Retard de Chasse	_Beaumont Sculp._
72.	Port de Mer	103.	Course de Bague Flamande	
73.	L'Écurie de la Poste	104.	Defilée de Cavallerie	____
74.	La Fontaine du Dauphin	105.	La Moisson	_Laurent Sculp._
75.	La Buvette des Cavaliers	106.	Le Repos	_Beaumont f._
76.	Les Bucherons	107.	La Pêche	____
77.	Le Quartier des Vivandiers	108.	Les Nageurs	____
78.	Le Départ des Cavaliers	109.	Halte de Cavallerie	____
79.	L'Écurie Flammande	110.	Halte de Cavallerie	_J.P. le Bas Sculp_
80.	Départ pour La Chasse a l'Oiseau	111.	Le Marechal en Exercice	_Beaumont f._
81.	La Grotte de l'Abbreuvoir	112.	Halte Flamande	____
82.	L'Écurie du Manège	113.	Vue d'Hollande	_C.N. Cochin Sculp._
83.	L'Abbreuvoir flammande	114.	Accident de Voyage	____
84.	Petite Meute de Chiens	115.	Des Cavaliers dont un est debout	_la Rocher fec. Danckerts vend_
85.	Petite partie de Chasse	116.	Manege devant une Grotte	_Danckerts f. e vend_
86.	Délassement de Troupes	117.	Le Retour du Marché	_R. Strange Sculps._
87.	Partie de Chasse pour le Vol	118.	La Soirée d'Été	_J.P. le Bas Sc._
88.	Devalisement d'Equipage	119.	La Matinée du Printems	____
89.	La Marchande de Canards			
90.	La Chasse a l'Italienne	_le Bas Sculp._		
91.	Le Pot au Lait			
92.	Les Sangliers forcés			
93.	Salle d'Officiers			
94.	Un Débarquement ou se trouve un Traineau avec un ballot marqué W.			
95.	Un Trompette, une Tente de Vivandier			
96.	Un Cavalier qui veut boire au milieu un Cheval blanc sellé			
97.	Le Rafraichissement de Cavaliers ou un Trompette sonne			
98.	Reste d'Armée décampée	_Beaumont 94_		
99.	Délassement de Laboureurs	_J. Roque Sculp._		
100.	Les Voituriers	_P. Filloul Sculp._		
101.	Halte Espagnole	_Jacq. Aliamet sc._		

Guillaume IX fecit

Ludwig Emil Grimm (see p. 161), represent another strength of the collection. The working papers of some of the artists named above are also kept here. Under the directorship of Erich Herzog in the 1960s and 70s, modern accessions increased substantially. Herzog systematically acquired prints and drawings of high quality by the group of artists called 'Die Brücke' (The Bridge), Ernst Ludwig Kirchner, Erich Heckel, and others. He was also interested in abstract art. Collections of the printed works of Willi Baumeister, Wols, Ernst Wilhelm Nay and Fritz Winter are almost complete. _Les_

Phénomènes, a large work by Jean Dubuffet with a total of 362 lithographs in 24 albums was purchased in 1963. Systematic acquisitions of this kind in specific areas of modern and contemporary art are no longer possible due to the reduced availability of funds. Representative examples can merely document individual trends today.

The largest part of the collection besides graphic art consists of about 4,500 architectural drawings. These are mainly by the architects in the service of the Hessian princes, e.g. the members of the du Ry family of architects, Heinrich Christoph Jussow, Johann Conrad Bromeis and Julius Eugen Ruhl. They document major royal projects in Kassel, Wilhelmshöhe and Wilhelmsthal. Besides the Staatsarchiv Marburg (state archive) and the Plankammer Potsdam (plans archive), the Collection of Prints and Drawings is the most important documentation centre for research on the history of architecture in Hesse.

A separate *Kupferstichkabinett* (print room) open to the public was not established in Kassel until late. Opened on 4 October 1931 as part of the Staatliche Kunstsammlungen (state art collections), the print room was set up at the same time as the art library in the Torwache (gate house), built by von Jussow near the Hessische Landesmuseum. The original core collection of about 20,000 prints was assembled from various sources. The most valuable items came from the landgraves' collections. The volumes of pasted prints had been loan deposits in the art gallery since 1916. Evidently Georg Gronau, the director at the time, had already been aiming to set up a print room. In 1931 precious old

master drawings were transferred from the Wilhelmshöhe palace library to the newly established print room. The Kassel Academy of Art handed over drawings and source materials collected since 1777 for teaching purposes. Many items on the history of Hesse, such as topographic views, portraits, construction drawings and military materials were contributed by the Hessisches Landesmuseum and a deposit of the Verein für hessische Geschichte und Landeskunde (Hessian History and Areal Studies Society).

The print room's late foundation date is enough to indicate that graphic art – compared to the great collection areas in Kassel of the art cabinet, the paintings and the antiquities – always played a rather marginal role. There is evidence that the landgraves of Hesse had collected prints since the 17th century. However, as opposed to their other collection areas, there was never an enthusiastic art lover to devote his connoisseurship particularly to this area. There was thus less of a collection of graphic art and more of a purpose-oriented acquisition of a repertory of paintings from the start. Nevertheless, each of the landgraves left his mark on the collection in connection with his special area of interest.

As in many royal graphic collections, the beginnings of the landgraves' print room can be found in portraiture. Portraits were commissioned to provide effective publicity for the family. In addition, the *contrefaits* of famous personalities, rulers, intellectuals, artists and exotic figures were also appreciated. The demand for this kind of visual information was satisfied most easily and economically by printing. Furthermore, maps were necessary for the administration of the territory. Devotional prints served religious needs. A fine print of the Man of Sorrows from the *Engraved Passion* by Dürer (illus. below) is inscribed on the unusually wide border: "My help cometh from the Lord, Eleonora Katharin z Hessen née PBR." This engraving from the property of Eleonora Katharina von Pfalz-Zweibrücken-Cleeburg, a daughter-in-law of Landgrave Moritz, is one of the oldest prints in the collection that can be linked to a member of the landgraves' family. Detailed information on the landgraves' collection of engravings is not available until the Kunsthaus inventory of 1747. Landgrave Karl had the Ottoneum, originally a theatre, made into an art gallery in 1696 for his encyclopaedic

Albrecht Dürer, Man of Sorrows, from the Engraved Passion, 1509

Albrecht Dürer, St Martin, about 1493

collections. It included a room for graphic media. Besides maps and topographical views, the inventory lists an random series of pictures of festivals and pageantry, illuminations, fireworks, burials, portraits, apparitions in the heavens and wonders of nature, as well as many plans that document the building activities of Landgrave Karl. A large number of drawings and prints was acquired in connection with the Hercules monument and its famous fountains built by Karl. These include views of great Italian gardens and various elevations for "water machines" and "artificial waterworks." Original works of graphic art, on the other hand, such as by Dürer, Lucas van Leyden and Callot, were bound and kept with the books in the mathematical cabinet.

Compared to this rather arbitrary and general assortment, the collection of Wilhelm VIII, the actual founder of the Kassel art gallery, seems to have been built up more systematically. Documented in the inventory of his estate of 1760, it was kept as a part of his private cabinet library in the landgraves' palace. Although here again maps, plans of battles and architectural drawings formed part of the collection, the emphasis was on prints after paintings. They served this lover of paintings as an informative reference library for his acquisitions. As in

Wilhelm's gallery, Flemish and Dutch artists were especially well represented. Selected prints, such as engravings after Italian paintings also appear, and from 1746 on Wilhelm acquired a complete set of prints after Watteau's paintings. Like his father Karl, Wilhelm VIII had original works of graphic art play a subordinate role only.

Following Wilhelm VIII, who had assigned his agents to fill the gaps in the print collection with selective acquisitions, Landgrave Friedrich II seems to have continued this practice. As the hereditary prince he had appointed de Mann, the Hessian envoy in The Hague, to look for missing Rembrandt etchings and Rubens engravings. In 1771 Friedrich bought the complete prints of Hogarth and in 1776/77 on his trip to Italy he received all the etchings of Piranesi as a gift from the Pope. These etchings, in a particularly splendid binding, are kept in the Weissenstein Wing of Schloss Wilhelmshöhe.

Unlike his predecessors, Wilhelm IX was less interested in enlarging the collection than in reorganising it. He had his Hanau library and parts of his father's cabinet library moved to his newly built palace, Schloss Wilhelmshöhe, where a library was set up in the *corps de logis* on the second storey. The court librarian Wilhelm Strieder was assigned to reorganise the collections of books and engravings. For each of the print portfolios organised according to schools and names of artists he made a table of contents. Wilhelm IX seems to have followed this reorganisation closely, for in the volume of prints after the paintings of Wouwermans he wrote and signed the list himself (see p. 163).

The descendants of Wilhelm IX did not add to the holdings of the Wilhelmshöhe palace library. It remained untouched until the first loans were deposited in the art gallery in 1916 and most of the remaining drawings and pasted albums were transferred to the newly founded print room in 1931. The core collection of old pasted volumes and master drawings still determines the character of today's Collection of Prints and Drawings. They afford the visitor an insight into the organisation and function of historical print collections and form a charming contrast to the high-quality new acquisitions in the area of modern art since 1931.

Albrecht Dürer

1471 Nuremberg – 1528 Nuremberg

Melencolia I, 1514
engraving, 24 x 18.5 cm
(trimmed to the edges of the printed plate)
from the collection of the landgraves,
Inv. no. GS 10499

Melencolia I dates from one of
Dürer's most productive periods,
when he was more intensely occupied
with printed works than with painting. Often considered together with
his engravings of St Jerome in his
Study and Knight, Death and Devil,
it belongs to the trio known as his
Master Engravings. Large in size,

expert in the mastery of the technique,
and "complex and meaningful in
iconography" (Panofsky), they number
among Dürer's most famous works.
This engraving may have come out of
one of the two disassembled volumes
filled with "all kinds of copperplate
prints by Albrecht Durer" that had
been in the landgraves' collection as
early as under Landgrave Karl.

Ever since Classical antiquity,
melancholy had been regarded as the
disposition of those who seek the
meaning of life. It is therefore assumed
that by making the connection between geometry and melancholy
Dürer created an "intellectual self-
portrait" (Panofsky).   *SH*

Paolo Veronese

1528 Verona – 1588 Venice

Study for an
Enthroned Venezia, 1576
graphite, pen and brown ink, wash,
24.8 x 20.6 cm
purchased 1939, Inv. no. GS 1124

After the fire in the Doge's Palace in 1574, the Venetian senate commissioned the city's most famous artists, including Veronese, to design new painted decorations for the representative rooms. This design is for the octagonal ceiling painting of the Sala del Collegio, where the Doge's visitors wait for an audience. The upper part of the preliminary drawing shows an enthroned Venezia in an octagonal frame distributing symbols of honour and being assisted by cupids. The recipients are shown as half-figures seen from behind, as they are cut off by the lower edge of the frame. Below the design, which is foreshortened in a pronounced view from below because of its function, Veronese drew Venezia's pose a second time. Proposals for inscriptions in the room and an architectural detail complete the page. The realised version of the ceiling painting deviates considerably from this design.

CL

The famous Dutch engraver Goltzius travelled to Rome in 1591 in order to perfect his art by studying and copying Classical works of art. He presumably planned a cycle of engravings after the most famous ancient sculptures. Just three prints were completed, however, appearing only posthumously in 1617. These include the rear view of the Farnese Hercules. Goltzius presumably chose this view in order to show the three apples of the Hesperides that the hero is holding in his hand behind his back. They stand for his virtues. *CL*

Hendrick Goltzius
1558 Meulebeke – 1617 Haarlem

The Farnese Hercules
Seen From the Back, about 1592
engraving, 40.5 x 29.4 cm (copperplate);
41.7 x 30.1 cm (paper)
from the landgraves' collection; Goltzius
album, fol. 89

The Farnese Hercules, a Roman copy of a Greek original by Lysippos, was found in Rome in 1546. Into the 19th century the sculpture was considered an exemplary, perfect, strong male body and was therefore often copied.

Roelant Savery
1576 Courtrai – 1639 Utrecht

Trees on the Shore, about 1610
graphite, black chalk, brown and grey wash,
blue and brown watercolour;
27.1 x 37.1 cm
from the landgraves' collection,
Inv. no. GS 5059

Towards the end of the 16th century it became common among the Flemish painters to depict the local forest. As opposed to the landscape views, the forest pieces were usually close-ups and enhanced with only a

bit of depth. One important precursor of this genre was the tree studies by Pieter Brueghel the Elder. They had a lasting influence on Savery as well as Paul Bril and Jan Brueghel the Elder. Savery, who spent some time at the court of Rudolf II in Prague, where studies of nature details were very much in demand, is considered a pioneer of the naturalistic approach to landscape around 1600. The appeal of this drawing with its unassuming motif is in the lively draughtsmanship and the economical use of accents set in chalk and watercolour to capture the sunlight and bring movement into the web of foliage. *CL*

Johann Liss

about 1597 Oldenburg, Harz (?) –
1631 Verona

Morra Players in an Osteria Garden,
about 1620
graphite, black and white chalk on brown
paper, 22.4 x 34.2 cm
purchased 1899, Inv. no. GS 1375

The corpus of drawings by Johann Liss, who is one of the few German painters of the early Baroque period, is small. Among the few drawings that can definitely be attributed to him is this preliminary drawing for his painting of *The Morra Game* in the Kassel collection (see p. 98).

It shows all kinds of people who have gathered in the garden of an osteria. The central group is enjoying a game of morra, in which the number of fingers that the players hold out should correspond to a number that is suddenly called.

In the painting Liss reduces the number of figures and concentrates on this group alone. He also changes the horizontal format into a vertical one in order to underscore the intensity of the scene. According to the biographer Joachim von Sandrart, drinking scenes by Liss were very popular with art lovers. His light draughtsmanship shows the influence of Venetian art. *CL*

Giovanni Francesco Guerniero
about 1665 Rome – 1745 Rome

Design for the Octagon
on the Karlsberg, 1713
graphite, pen and black ink, wash
65.5 x 48.3 cm
from the landgraves' collection
Inv. no. GS 5547

Landgrave Karl had very expensive
fountains and waterworks built on the
slope above Weissenstein Palace from
1701 on. They were to culminate in a
lookout terrace. He had made the
acquaintance of the architect Guerniero, who was to execute the project,
on his trip to Italy in 1699. Guerniero
recorded the landgrave's grandiose
plans, according to which the waterworks were to extend to the palace
and even into the residency of Kassel,
in a cycle of engravings entitled Delineatio montis. The only two design
drawings that have been preserved
concern the Octagon. It was not until
1713 that it was to be crowned to
enhance its effect. This plan projects
two pyramids with Hercules and

Minerva. Only a plainer version with
one pyramid was executed, topped by
a monumental copy of the Farnese
Hercules.   CL

Johann Heinrich Tischbein
the Elder
1722 Haina – 1789 Kassel

Calypso's Feast, 1756
graphite, pen and grey-brown ink,
watercolour
17.2 x 21.4 cm
Inv. no. GS 447f

Johann Heinrich Tischbein the Elder
is one of the most famous members
of a large dynasty of artists. In 1754
Landgrave Wilhelm VIII appointed
him as his court painter and commissioned him to paint, among other projects, overdoors for the newly built
little Rococo palace of Wilhelmsthal.
Its upper storey was to be decorated
with a cycle of the adventures of Telemachus from the popular didactic
romance by Fénelon. The design for
Calypso's Feast provides the framework of the plot. Telemachus is stran-
ded on the nymph's island and is telling her about his adventures at an
intimate meal. The threatening conflict, Telemachus's choice between
Minerva, the goddess of wisdom, and

Venus, the goddess of love, is already suggested by the intimacy of the scene. The preference of the Rococo for pleasing erotic scenes is also readily apparent.   CL

Johann Martin von Rohden

1778 Kassel – 1868 Rome

Woman Praying on a Street in Tivoli, about 1805
pencil, 19.7 x 27.2 cm
purchased 1972, Inv. no. GS 1972/27

Tivoli, with its famous waterfalls, important ancient ruins and Renaissance villas with their gardens and fountains, was one of the most popular places for excursions into the environs of Rome. Besides those travelling for study, artists were attracted to it ever since the 17th century, repeatedly depicting the beauties of the place. The Kassel landscape painter J.M. von Rohden, who spent most of his life in Italy, often stayed in Tivoli too. In this pencil drawing, which is composed like a painting, he did not chose one of the usual motifs but an unspectacular spot in the centre of town, where a woman kneels in prayer in front of an altar. His profound piety links Rohden to the Nazarenes, who were active in Rome from 1810 on and tried to reform art on the basis of Christian faith.   CL

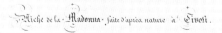

This drawing was made in 1910, when Heckel and Kirchner were finding their way to a harder and more angular form of expression after the soft style of the early Brücke years. Kirchner suggests the thin, still undeveloped body of the girl with spare, hard, contour lines that are continually broken off. The lines form a strict structure revealing a high degree of concentration, yet without losing the lightness of the artist's touch. As opposed to precise academic studies of nudes drawn from posed models, Kirchner's works try to capture his models spontaneously and directly through their movements.   *SH*

Ernst Ludwig Kirchner

1880 Aschaffenburg –
1938 Frauenkirch

Wildboden near Davos
Marzella with her Hair Down, 1910
reed pen and brush, black ink on
yellow paper, 42.7 x 30.3 cm
purchased 1964, Inv. no. MG 1964/43

The Collection of Prints and Drawings has a small selection of Kirchner's drawings that is representative for his entire production. No other artist of his time left behind as large a corpus of drawings. His drawings, which he himself considered "the purest and most beautiful part of his work," also provide an approach to his paintings and prints. The subject of the nude continues throughout all the phases of his work and particularly determined his early years with the Brücke group. His models were often the girlfriends and friends of the Brücke artists. From 1909 these included young pubescent girls.

Erich Heckel

1883 Döbeln, Saxony – 1970 Radolfzell

Portrait of a Man, 1919
coloured woodcut, 66.5 x 48.5 cm
(paper)
purchased 1965
Inv. no. MG 1965/121

Coloured woodcuts by Erich Heckel represent an apogee of the art of the German Expressionist woodcut. He had already worked in depth on this technique as early as the Brücke period from 1905 to 1913. This portrait links up directly with the late expressive woodcuts made when he was still in the Brücke group.

The print entitled Portrait of a Man dating from 1919 is also a self-portrait. Heckel portrays himself in a melancholy contemplative pose, his hands folded and pressed against his chin. The inner contours of the face and hands are rendered with free irregular lines. On the block that printed the drawing in black, Heckel superimposed another block, cut apart and coloured, to print the coloured planes in a second step. Paint was thinly applied on this block with a brush or paintbrush, causing the white of the paper to show through and the brushstrokes to remain visible. In this way each print differs in colour and texture and acquires the unique status of an original. *SH*

Ernst Wilhelm Nay
1902 Berlin – 1968 Cologne

The Shepherd, 1948
pencil, gouache, 26.5 x 21.5 cm
purchased 1962, Inv. no. MG 1962/44

The small gouache of The Shepherd is closely related in form to a painting of the same subject that exists in three only slightly differing versions. The second version is also in the collections of the Staatliche Museen Kassel and is exhibited in the Neue Galerie. The painting and the gou-

ache belong to the so-called "Hecate pictures" that Nay made between 1945 and 1948 after he returned to Germany from the war. Hecate is a goddess of the underworld. She is the mistress of all nocturnal evil deeds, witchcraft and the brewing of poisons. Two paintings by Nay, Daughters of Hecate I and II, lent the dark goddess's name to the entire creative phase. The "Hecate pictures," in which Nay came to terms with his wartime experiences, mark a turning point in his work from figurative to abstract art. Nay combines a constantly recurring repertoire of forms into two-dimensional colour compositions that still suggest figurative elements. Titles from ancient mythology or Biblical history added later allow free associations and vividly demonstrate the timelessness of myth. *SH*

H. Cosmographie

Jean Dubuffet

1901 Le Havre – 1985 Paris

Cosmographie, 1958
print IVX from album 4
Le Preneur d'empreintes
(the collector of prints)
from Les Phénomènes (The Phenomena),
1958–1962
lithograph, 63.3 x 45 cm (paper)
puchased 1963, Inv. no. MG 1963/24,
GS 16075

Cosmography is from a cycle of 362
prints called Les Phénomènes by Jean
Dubuffet of which the Collection of
Prints and Drawings has the complete
set. The cycle represents the apogee
and the conclusion of Dubuffet's
lithographic works. He worked on it
from January 1958 to April 1959;
publication was completed in 1962.
The large album was originally planned as a sample collection of various
materials, surfaces and textures without artistic content of its own. For the
first pages Dubuffet made rubbings
from surfaces of walls, floors and the
like and transferred them to the stone

or zinc plate. In subsequent prints he
experimented with tracing techniques
and oxidation processes directly on
the stone or zinc plate and printed the
structures in superimposed and partly
coloured form. For the last albums he
cut up the patterns in order to assem-
ble them into collages and print them
again. Simply numbered consecutively
at first, the prints were later organised
by subject in 24 albums. The themes
of the albums, such as Basic Concepts,
Geography, and The Anarchitect,
create additional associations that put
the prints into a larger systematic context as an inventory of the materials
of the world.   *SH*

Wols

1913 Berlin – 1951 near Paris

Three Figures on the Beach,
1939/40
pen and black ink, watercolour,
24.2 x 30.6 cm
purchased in 1965, Inv. no. MG 1965/74

The oeuvre of Wols, whose real name
was Alfred Otto Wolfgang Schulze,
had a decisive influence on Tachist art
and Art informel after 1945. The
Collection of Prints and Drawings
owns almost all of his printed works
and a small selection of early watercolours influenced by Surrealism.
They were made in 1939–40 when
Wols spent time in various internment
camps in the south of France. "One
tells one's little earthly fables on little
pieces of paper," was Wols's terse comment on these works. Wols drew
them with a sure hand in pen and ink
directly on paper without any under-
drawings, and coloured them with
transparently applied watercolours.

Fabulous composite creatures move weightlessly in a kind of dream landscape. The drawings in the Collection of Prints and Drawings were probably part of a selection of watercolours and drawings that Wols gave the writer Kay Boyle in France to take to America in the vain hope of emigrating there himself. In 1942 some of these works were exhibited for the first time in New York in the Betty Parsons Gallery.   *SH*

to achieve different effects by changing the technique. This variety constitutes the special appeal of the portfolio. Baselitz has been turning his motifs upside down ever since 1969 in order to emphasise the artistic as opposed to the subject content. The motifs nevertheless remain clearly identifiable. Ever since 1974 the subject of the eagle has not relinquished its hold on the artist. It reflects his creative development in exemplary fashion.   *CL*

Georg Baselitz
1938 Deutschbaselitz

print 11 of the Adler (Eagle)
portfolio, 1974
woodcut, partly overpainted,
44.8 x 34.7 cm (paper)
purchased 1998, municipal property,
AZG 1998/8, Inv. no. SK 81

Prints rank highly among the works of Georg Baselitz, whose achievements in the 1960s were decisive for the revival of traditional techniques. This intense preoccupation is reflected in the Adler (Eagle) portfolio. It is the first portfolio by the artist containing several techniques appearing side by side. While the eagle motif is repeated from one page to the next, the aim is

Library

The library of the Staatliche Museen Kassel is a non-circulating collection specialising on the collection areas of the state museums of Hesse. The reading room in the Kirchflügel (church wing) of Schloss Wilhelmshöhe is open to visitors.

Library holdings currently number about 90,000 volumes – with annual accessions of about 2,500 volumes. About 575 journals and series are on standing order. The majority of the new accessions is acquired through world-wide exchange programmes with other museums and institutions.

The subjects collected are: art history (with the emphasis on 17th-century Netherlandish art, German and Italian Baroque painting, and 19th-century art), artists' monographs, as well as exhibition, museum and auction catalogues (Christie's and Sotheby's auction catalogues are on standing order; there is also a large collection of historic auction catalogues). Classical archaeology is further collection area.

The special libraries of the departments of minor arts and sculpture, folklore and folk art, ancient and prehistoric history, of the Deutsches Tapetenmuseum (German Wallpaper Museum) and the Museum für Astronomie und Technikgeschichte (Museum of Astronomy and the History of Technology) are in the Hessische Landesmuseum. All of these library collections, with a few exceptions, are listed in the catalogue of the museum library in Schloss Wilhelmshöhe and can be ordered and consulted in the reading room.

Opening Hours:
Monday–Thursday   9:00 – 13:00
Friday   8:00 – 12:00

Ballhaus
at Schloss Wilhelmshöhe

The Ballhaus, a former ballroom, in front of the northern wing of the palace came about in 1828–1830 when radical alterations were made to the court theatre. Jérôme Bonaparte, the regent of the Kingdom of Westphalia 1807–1813, had had this theatre built in order to have exclusively French comedies and comic operas performed next to his residential palace, which he renamed "Napoleonshöhe." He commissioned Leo von Klenze (1784–1864) for the design and realisation. From 1808 to 1810 under strict "economic considerations" the architect built his first project here. The main entrance under a Tuscan portico was on the side facing the park. The king entered his theatre through the portal on

the palace side, still extant at the time.

The alterations that turned it into a "dance hall for the public" were instigated by Prince Elector Wilhelm II (1821–1831). Johann Conrad Bromeis (1788–1855) was the court architect he commissioned. The royal box (today the gallery) was preserved, as was the portico on the street side. The building was given new windows, and one level room replaced the stalls and stage. An orchestra gallery was inserted at the acoustically most favourable spot above the royal box under a new and higher barrel vault. The splendid wall and ceiling paintings, with ancient gods in decorative wall panels, East Indian birds along an arabesque frieze and flower garlands

Ballhaus, interior, "From Coast to Coast" exhibition, 1992

decorating the panel ceiling, lend the room a cheerful and festive Arcadian atmosphere. Structural security measures, conservation and restoration work in 1975–1985 ensured that this major historic monument could be opened to the public. Since 1986 it has housed temporary exhibitions by the Staatliche Museen Kassel during the summer months.

Exhibitions in the Ballhaus:

Models and Drawings of Ancient Buildings 1986, Historicism 1987, Etruscan Painting 1988, Karl Rumpf 1989, G. Möhwald 1990, Apollo and Athena 1991, From Coast to Coast 1992, Crystals out of the Fire 1993, Ferdinand Tellgmann; Werra Ware from Enkhuizen 1994, Travel in a Box 1995, The Most Elegant Ruins of Rome 1996, Hercules 1997, Kassel Silver 1998, Building Blocks; Turquoise and Azure 1999

Ballhaus, facade

Schloss Wilhelmshöhe, Weissenstein Wing

State Palaces and Gardens Administration of Hesse

Historic Representative and Residential Rooms

34131 Kassel-Wilhelmshöhe
Tel.: 05 61/9 35 71 00
Fax: 05 61/9 35 71 11

Opening Hours:

Tue–Sun March to Oct 10:00–17:00, last guided tour 16:00;
Nov to Feb 10:00–16:00, last guided tour 15:00.
Closed Mondays except on public holidays.
Closed 24–26 Dec, 31 Dec, 1 Jan

Guided Tours:

Historic representative and residential rooms on the main and first floor (duration 45 min). Admission: adults DM 7, concessions DM 5, groups of 15 or more DM 5 per person, schools DM 44, kindergarten groups DM 22, families DM 19. Annual ticket: adults DM 55, children DM 33, families DM 143. Verbundkarte (joint ticket for Weissenstein Wing, Löwenburg, Hercules, Grosses Gewächshaus [Large Glasshouse] and Schloss Wilhelmsthal): DM 21. Combi-ticket for individuals and families for Schloss Wilhelmshöhe and the park (Nordhessischer Verkehrsverbund, Staatliche Museen Kassel, Verwaltung der Staatlichen Schlösser und Gärten Hessen), includes public transport: adults DM 10 / DM 20 (incl. Löwenburg, Grosses Gewächshaus and Hercules); families DM 25 / DM 50.

The Weissenstein Wing was the first south pavilion of today's Schloss Wilhelmshöhe to be erected. It was built in 1786–1798 according to designs by the architects S.L. Du Ry and H.C. Jussow. It is the only part of the building left after the destruction of World

The bathroom dating from 1825, with its marble tub inserted into the floor, and has wall panels painted with landscape motifs imitating Classical antiquity.

Jérôme Bonaparte's desk by F.Wichmann, 1810/11. After Napoleon's victory, his brother Jérôme occupied the residence temporarily and changed the furnishings to suit his taste.

War II that still has the original floor plans and historic interior decoration.

Commissioned by Landgrave Wilhelm IX, later Elector Wilhelm I, the elegant simplicity of the residential apartments documents the Neo-Classical taste of its patron, who was clearly distancing himself from the Baroque splendour displayed by his predecessors. The turn towards the more private character of an electoral residential palace of the late 18th and early 19th centuries is noticeable rather than that of the severe court ceremonial of the Age of Absolutism, aimed at the public representation of sovereign power, which had lost its significance.

The precious Louis Seize and Empire style furniture and the numerous marble sculptures copying Classical originals are some of the most important examples of art around 1800.   UB

Wilhelmshöhe Palace Park

Hercules, Octagon, Platform and Pyramid

Opening Hours: 15 March–15 Oct, 10:00–17:00 daily.
Admission: adults DM 3.50, concessions DM 2.50, families DM 9, schools DM 32, kindergarten groups DM 16. Verbundkarte (joint ticket for Weissenstein, Hercules, Löwenburg, Grosses Gewächshaus and Schloss Wilhelmsthal) DM 21. Combi-ticket for Schloss Wilhelmshöhe and park, see Weissenstein Wing above.

Fountains and Waterworks

Guided tours of the fountains from the Hercules, Cascades, Steinhöfer Waterfall, Teufelsbrücke (Devil's Bridge) and Aqueduct to the Great Fountain every Wed and Sun at 14:00

Schloss Wilhelmshöhe, here still with its central dome and connecting wings, in its setting in the Bergpark, with the Löwenburg and Hercules. Painting by Johann Erdmann Hummel, 1799/1800 (Staatliche Museen Kassel)

(duration 100 min.) from May to Oct. Meeting point: Octagon box office. Adults DM 10, concessions DM 7, families DM 25, schools and kindergarten groups (by reservation only) DM 40.

Palace Park

Guided tours "From Hercules to the Palace" (120 min.); "Around the Palace" (about 90 min.); prices upon request.

Special Events

"Illuminated Waterworks" at the Hercules, Aqueduct and Great Fountain after dark each first Saturday of the month from June to Sept. Free admission. "Palace by Candlelight" presents the palace rooms of the Weissenstein

View up the Cascades to the Hercules

The Large Glasshouse, facade

Wing in candlelight on days when the fountains are illuminated in the park, each first Saturday of the month, evenings from June to Sept. Admission: adults DM 7, concessions DM 5.

Schoss Wilhelmshöhe is embedded in the largest mountain park in Europe today. The original Baroque grounds, with an axial perspective extending from the landgraves' palace along the 250-metre-long cascade up to the gigantic Hercules on the hill that can still be seen today, was designed by the Italian architect G.F. Guerniero at the beginning of the 18th century. Under Landgraves Friedrich II (1760–1785) and Wilhelm IX (1785–1821) additional features around the Baroque axis of the Cascades took advantage of the topographic features to create an extensive idealised natural landscape with surprising perspectives and numerous attractions for visitors. These include an artificially created 'Roman' aqueduct, waterfalls, thrilling canyons, dizzying bridges, Neo-Classical temples, exotic and pseudo-medieval buildings. The mountain park, with

its great forest stand, park buildings, Löwenburg and Large Glasshouse, and the Weissenstein Wing with its historic rooms on display, have been administered by the Verwaltung Staatliche Schlösser und Gärten Hessen (State Palaces and Gardens Administration of Hesse), succeeding the Prussian Palace Administration, since 1946.   UB

Large Glasshouse
Botanical Exhibition

Opening Hours:
From the end of Nov. to 1 May inclusive, 10:00–17:00 daily. Admission: adults DM 3.50, concessions DM 2.50, families DM 9, schools DM 32, kindergarten groups DM 16, season ticket DM 10; green ticket (annual ticket with Insel Siebenbergen) DM 27.50; Verbundkarte (joint ticket for Weissenstein, Hercules, Löwenburg, Large Glasshouse and Schloss Wilhelmsthal) DM 21; combi-ticket for Schloss Wilhelmshöhe and park, see Weissenstein Wing above.

Elector Wilhelm II had J.C. Bromeis build a glasshouse for his rare collection of exotic plants in 1822–23. The lightness of its iron-and-glass construction and the bright light indoors make the botanical exhibition building very attractive. Its rich, partly tropical world of plants with exotic birds continues to fascinate visitors today.

Löwenburg in the Wilhelmshöhe Palace Park

Opening Hours:
Tues–Sun March to Oct 10:00–17:00, last guided tour 16:00;
Nov–Feb 10:00–16:00, last guided tour 15:00. Closed Mondays, except on public holidays. Closed 24–26 Dec, 31 Dec, 1 Jan.

Guided Tours:
Residential apartments in the ladies' and gentlemen's wings, royal stables, chapel, armoury (duration 45 min.).

Admission: same as Weissenstein Wing (see above). Verbundkarte (joint ticket for Weissenstein, Hercules, Löwenburg, Large Glasshouse and Schloss Wilhelmsthal) DM 21; combi-ticket for Schloss Wilhelmshöhe and park, see Weissenstein Wing above.

Landgrave Wilhelm IX had the Löwenburg developed between 1793 and 1801 by H.C. Jussow as a picturesque focal point in the landscape park of Wilhelmshöhe. As though to conjure up ruling structures of old, the knight's castle appears on the outside as an invincible knight's castle, now a derelict ruin. Its apparent worthy old age seems to legitimise the seniority of the princely family and hence the right of the house of Hesse-Kassel to power. Actually, this was a period of intellectual and social change, when the divine right of kings and the absolute subordination of subjects were being challenged everywhere. The interior of the castle features unex-

The Löwenburg, one of the first buildings of Historicism in Germany

Bedroom in the knight's apartment in the gentlemen's wing of the Löwenburg

pectedly Baroque royal apartments to house the landgrave and his court. Besides the impressive armoury with weapons and knight's armour of the 16th and 17th centuries, and the cast-le chapel with the tomb of the patron, visitors can view the royal apartments in the ladies' and gentlemen's wings, which are partly historically furnish-ed, partly set up as a museum.   *UB*

The armoury in the Löwenburg. In the centre is a set of armour for a horse and rider dating from the 16th century

Selected Bibliography

Collection of Antiquities

M. Bieber, *Die antiken Skulpturen und Bronzen*, Marburg 1915

E. Berger, *Antike Kunstwerke – Neuerwerbungen*, Kassel 1961

U. Höckmann, *Antike Bronzen*, Kassel 1973

U. Sinn, *Antike Terrakotten*, Kassel 1977

Aufklärung und Klassizismus, exh. cat. Kassel 1979

F. Naumann, *Antiker Schmuck*, Kassel 1980

P. Gercke et al, *Funde aus der Antike – Sammlung Paul Dierichs*, Kassel 1981

M. Boosen, *Antike Gläser*, Kassel 1984

P. Gercke – B. Hamborg, *Antike Münzen*, Kassel 1985

Chr. Höcker, *Antike Gemmen*, Kassel 1988

K. Yfantidis, *Antike Gefäße*, Kassel 1990

P. Gercke et al, *APOLLON und ATHENA*, Kassel 1991

A. Felgenhauer, *Ägyptische und Ägyptisierende Kunstwerke*, Kassel 1996

P. Gercke et al, *Samos – Die Kasseler Grabung 1984*, Kassel 1996

R. Busz - P. Gercke (eds), *Türkis und Azur*, Kassel 1999

Old Masters Art Gallery

S. Causid, *Verzeichnis der Hochfürstlich = Heßischen Gemählde = Sammlung in Cassel*, Cassel 1783 (reprint 1799)

O. Eisenmann, *Katalog der Königlichen Gemälde-Galerie zu Cassel*, Cassel 1888

H. Vogel, *Katalog der Staatlichen Gemäldegalerie zu Kassel*, Kassel 1958

E. Herzog – J. M. Lehmann, *Unbekannte Schätze der Kasseler Gemälde-Galerie*, Kassel 1968

E. Herzog, *Die Gemäldegalerie der Staatlichen Kunstsammlungen Kassel*, Hanau 1969

J. M. Lehmann, *Staatliche Kunstsammlungen Kassel*, cat. I, *Italienische, französische und spanische Gemälde des 16.–18. Jahrhunderts*, Fridingen 1980

B. Schnackenburg, *Flämische Meister in der Kasseler Gemäldegalerie*, Kassel 1985 (2. ed. 1989)

J. M. Lehmann, *Italienische, französische und spanische Meister in der Kasseler Gemäldegalerie*, Kassel 1986 (2. ed. 1991)

G. J. M. Weber, *Stillleben alter Meister in der Kasseler Gemäldegalerie*, Melsungen 1989

B. Schnackenburg, *Staatliche Museen Kassel, Gemäldegalerie Alte Meister*, collections cat., text and plate vols, Mainz 1996

A. Schneckenburger-Broschek, *Altdeutsche Malerei, Die Tafelbilder und Altäre des 14.–16. Jahrhunderts*, Eurasburg 1997

Collection of Prints and Drawings

L. Oehler, *Niederländische Zeichnungen des 16. bis 18. Jahrhunderts*, Fridingen 1979

Herkules, *Tugendheld und Herrscherideal*, exh. cat. ed. Chr. Lukatis and H. Ottomeyer, Munich 1997

Heinrich Christoph Jussow (1754 – 1825), *Ein hessischer Architekt des Klassizismus*, exh. cat. ed. H. Ottomeyer and Chr. Lukatis, Kassel 1999

Mit Pinsel, Feder und Stift – Meisterzeichnungen der Graphischen Sammlung. ed. Staatl. Museen Kassel, Chr. Lukatis and H. Ottomeyer, Wolfratshausen 2000

Index of Artists

MUSEUMSVEREIN KASSEL E.V.

Support the work of the Staatliche Museen Kassel:
become a member!

Enjoy the following benefits:

● free entry into all institutions administered by the
  Staatliche Museen Kassel, including special exhibitions
● free mailings of the quarterly programme of the
  Staatliche Museen Kassel
● free mailings of invitations to all museum events
● free special tours for members
● one to two day art-tours within Germany and abroad

Enrol at the cashier's or museum's offices:

Museumsverein Kassel e.V.
c/o Staatliche Museen Kassel
Schloss Wilhelmshöhe
Postfach 41 04 20
D-34066 Kassel
Tel.: 0561/93 77-7
Fax: 0561/93 77-666
e-mail: smk-info@hz.uni-kassel.de